RESET FAMILIES

Building Social and Emotional Skills while Avoiding Nagging and Power Struggles

Sharon Aller, DTL
Greg Benner, PhD
Angel Finsrud

www.resetfamilies.org
Curriculum & Parent Handbook available

Copyright © 2018 Sharon Aller, DTL, Greg Benner, PhD and
Angel Finsrud
All rights reserved
First Edition

PAGE PUBLISHING, INC.
New York, NY

First originally published by Page Publishing, Inc. 2018

ISBN 978-1-64350-227-4 (Paperback)
ISBN 978-1-64350-226-7 (Digital)

Printed in the United States of America

*To the parents and caregivers who have convinced
us that change and restoration are possible*

Contents

Introduction	Restorative Parenting: Balancing Strong Family Connections With Trust and Accountability	7
Chapter 1:	Leading Change in Your Family	9
Chapter 2:	Creating a Shared Family Vision	23
Chapter 3:	Strengthening Family Connections	46
Chapter 4:	Setting Clear Expectations	64
Chapter 5:	Integrating Expectations with Behavior Redirection	85
Chapter 6:	Focus on Restoration – Using Reset Effectively	110
Chapter 7:	Consequences as Teaching Tools	135
Chapter 8:	Rewards that Build Relationships	155
Afterword:	On Being Human, Restoring Connections, and Painting Pictures of Hope	171
Further Resources		173
References		191

Introduction

Restorative Parenting: Balancing Strong Family Connections With Trust and Accountability

We are pretty much convinced that parenting is the hardest job in the world. Parents are given the incredible responsibility of shaping the foundation on which an entire life will be built. Our kids are born with personalities, temperaments, strengths, and talents. As parents, it's our job to nurture their design and help them grow into responsible adults who will contribute to the world around them. That's no small task. Our approach to raising our children will influence so much of who they become. And yet, very few of us had any clue what we were getting into when we started out on this parenting journey. Sure, we may have had a list of things we would *never* do or allow, or ways we would *always* behave, but three months into sleep deprivation, failed attempts at figuring out why the baby is crying, and trying to figure out how to juggle life with a child, most of us quickly realized we were in over our head with this parenting thing.

Parenting is often much harder than we thought it was going to be. Or at the very least, we're not as good at this as we hoped. Some of us have children that are so challenging and demanding that teachers and social workers are sounding the alarm, but we feel we don't know how we can keep moving forward. Perhaps a few of us are blessed with an easier transition to parenthood. In that case, maybe it's not until the second child or the teen years come along that we realize this is hard work. No doubt parenting stretches us in ways we never imagined, but no matter where we're starting from, we can gain the skills to be the parent we really want to be. For most of us, that means we want to have a great relationship with our kids but still set limits that help them grow into responsible adults.

If you can relate to any of these challenges with parenting, you are not alone. The fact that you have opened this book indicates that when it comes to parenting, you believe that we all have things to learn. Your interest in parenting indicates you are willing to reflect on what you have gotten right as well as what you are not so proud of. Most importantly, it means you recognize the importance of the job you have as a caregiver. You understand that you only get one shot at raising your kids, and you want to do the best you can for them. Since this is the case, I would say your kids are pretty lucky to have you. It's impossible to get it all right when it comes to parenting, but being willing to learn and grow shows how committed you are to being the best parent you can be for your kids.

Who doesn't want a closer relationship with their child? In over thirty years of working with parents, we have found that parents absolutely want close relationships with their kids but struggle to find a practical response to the arguing, yelling, and chaos that is so destructive to the very thing they value most.

The Reset Families approach draws from research and best practices to help parents and caregivers create a family culture that nurtures connection even as we give our kids the correction and support they need. Reset Families is based on Positive Behavioral Intervention and Supports (PBIS), a proactive approach to establishing the behavioral supports and social culture needed for children to achieve social, emotional, and academic success.[1] It prepares you to teach your kids the lifelong skills they need to manage their own behavior, to own their mistakes, repair damage done, and move on. The result is a balance between relationships and accountability that builds trust and strengthens relationships.

Chapter 1

Leading Change in Your Family

Most of us are not prepared for the power struggles and challenges that often become a reality as we interact with our children. The phrase "the Terrible Twos" must have been born out of the sheer exasperation that many parents experience as they begin to realize that despite our best intentions and highest hopes, our kids won't always do what is good for them.

It's around these "Terrible Twos" that we begin to experience power struggles with our kids. Power struggles reveal themselves in familiar ways. We put our child to bed. She gets out of bed. We put her back to bed. She gives us a list of demands—one more story, a drink of water, one more trip to the bathroom. With high hopes we meet the needs our child has expressed and put her back to bed only the have her get up again. This situation often escalates until we become frustrated, hand out threats of consequences, slam the door, *or* perhaps we finally give in, allowing the child to snuggle on the couch or stay up just a little longer.

You may see this pattern repeat itself over climbing on bookshelves, not wanting to get in the car seat, or any other resisted request—you name it. And as kids get older, the struggles evolve into negotiations of TV time, homework, or bedtime. There may be parents out there who never get drawn into the struggle, but we haven't met them yet.

Why Power Struggles?

There has been a lot of work done to try and figure out how parents and children negatively interact in ways that often harm rather than build relationships. A researcher, James Patterson,[2] identified the Coercion Cycle. You might not be familiar with the term, but I bet you have experienced it. The Coercion Cycle recognizes that kids learn quickly how far to push to get our attention. After all, that is what they truly want from us. After repeated attempts to get our attention, they may engage in a minor infraction of the rules knowing that they will be "in trouble," but at least they will have our attention.

Parents are rarely ready for this and see it as defiant behavior from their child. The typical default reaction is to return threats to get compliance. You may have heard yourself say something like, "If you don't stop kicking the chair, I am going to send you to your room." If there is no response from the child, frustration sets in. You up your game by saying, "I said, quit that right now, and I mean it!" Often the child continues to ignore, and you are at the boiling point. You may say in a staccato voice, "Jonathan David, you are grounded. Go to your room." Your child jumps off the chair, objecting emphatically, "That's not fair." At this point you have been caught in the coercion cycle that is destructive to both of you. Our children learn that escalating, the behavior will result in more of our attention even though it means trouble. The negative spiral continues.

Nattering, nagging, and arguing frustrate both the parent and the child and result in a power struggle. The child becomes more assertive, and parents respond by becoming even more assertive. The situation escalates instead of deescalating or resolving. Often, this struggle results in frustration on the part of the parent who eventually just gives up so that there is a bit of peace and quiet.

When we give in, we inadvertently reinforce the child's negative behavior, we teach the child that if they resist long enough we will cave in to their demands, and the downward spiral continues.

I am certain that none of us entered the adventure of parenting picturing the days that we would be reduced to that angry parent, snapping at their child out of pure frustration. However, if we are honest, we can all look back to times when our interactions with our kids were far different from what we hoped or dreamed they would be.

Our desire is to help you learn new ways to respond to those frustrating times and to equip you with tools that will help you work toward making your family all you hoped it would be.

Change Starts with You

So where do we begin? One thing we believe about building a strong family is that no matter how good our skills may be, we need to balance skills with strong relationships as we interact with our kids. We all want negative behavior from our kids to stop, but it is important to remember that the beginning of effective discipline is relationship. It is the type of bond that develops over time based on the family culture we have created and the interactions that we use to sustain it.

In spite of all the great advice and best-laid plans, our kids seem to have the ability to drive us crazy at times. Our kids are our greatest joy, and at the same time they can push our buttons like no one else. How can such adorable creatures also be so demanding and at times downright defiant?

Often when we pick up a parenting book, what we really are looking for is a way to fix the way our kid is acting. I came across a comic with a mother holding the hand of her child, looking at him with a smile, and saying, "You are making it hard for me to be the parent I always thought I would be." We vow to ourselves that tomorrow we aren't going to yell at our kids to get them out of the house on time. Or that next time we won't give in just to get peace. But in the heat of the moment, when our kids aren't responding the way we hoped, before we know it we've reacted in a way we regret.

We hope to share tools, ideas, and inspiration that will help you become the parent you want to be, even when your children aren't behaving in the ways you expected. If you really want to begin to parent in an intentional way, regardless of how your kids are behaving, then the most important place to begin is by looking at yourself. The change in your family has to start with you!

Initiating Change

As you think about leading your family, it is important to acknowledge that you didn't walk into parenting with a blank slate. We all bring a box of tools with us into parenting. Some of our tools and habits are very valuable, but others get in the way of our success as parents. Take some time to think about what you have brought with you into your family. Look back at the family you grew up in. What have you learned from your family of origin that you want to incorporate in your own family? For some of us, it is easy to list the things we appreciated or value about the family we grew up in. For others, it may be hard to come up with even one thing you'd do the same way your parents did. Wherever you find yourself, reflecting on the way you were parented is valuable.

Once you have thought about your list, continue the process by thinking about some of the ways you were parented that you would like to change. As parents, we are flooded with parenting information. Before your child is even born you were probably inundated with information on how your baby was growing, what to eat, safe ways to sleep, best ways to feed, what brands to use—and the list goes on and on. As our kids grow, everywhere we turn people our offering advice. Your mother-in-law, the leaders at church, the school, and countless bloggers, talk-show hosts, and television programs are all shouting for your attention so they can give you good advice on parenting or trying to sell you something. It can be overwhelming. No wonder so many of us find ourselves parenting according to the way we were brought up, just doing what we see others do, or trying out what seems to work on reality TV shows.

Being pulled in so many directions can distract us from what is most important for our family. In the pages that follow, we will suggest ways you can be intentional in the way you respond to your kids so that the responses create positive, healthy, and safe home environments. We will offer strategies that build relationships while you teach your kids the skills to own their behavior choices, learn to repair damage done, and move on.

Talking about change is one thing, but change isn't change until something changes. In the following pages, we will explore ways to begin the change process in your family rather than remaining hostage to your past or the whim of each new parenting fad. A great place to start is by evaluating how you currently parent.

Know Your Default Parenting Style

Your default parenting style is a response that comes naturally or automatically. It is obvious especially when you are overwhelmed, angry, tired, or under pressure. Our default parenting style is derived from our genetics and environment. Our own particular style of parenting has evolved from a combination of inherited traits and experiences. Experiences that help form our default can be positive, like the patience of your father or the healthy food choices in your family. Or they can be derived from adverse experiences, like trauma we have experienced in our family of origin or previous relationships.

Ideally, we would rather make intentional, well-thought-out parenting decisions, but under pressure, our default styles often emerge. The tendency to slip into our default parenting style becomes an obstacle to moving from a reactive parenting style to intentional parenting. Intentional parenting happens when we begin making decisions about the kind of parent we want to be and then practice the habits and skills necessary to become that type of parent. Over time you can change your default parenting style. However, remember, it has taken years for this default to form, and it will take a while for you to begin to feel comfortable, even natural, with your new parenting responses. The first step in changing your negative defaults is to learn to identify your default style.

As you reflect on the way you were parented and evaluate your own approach to parenting, it may be helpful to consider which characteristics of the commonly referred to parenting styles most reflect how you tend to operate with your kids. Do you tend to let your kids figure things out on their own without a lot of involvement, or are you the type that expects your kids to do what you say when you say it? Do you show your child lots of love but find it hard to enforce rules? Do you believe that your kids need lots of love but at the same time you have to hold your kids accountable for family expectations? Is your life so busy with work or other activities that you find it difficult to focus on your kids?

Questions like these can help you determine if you are more of a permissive parent, an influential parent (authoritative), a disciplinarian (authoritarian), or an uninvolved parent. Keep in mind that none of us fits perfectly into any one of these styles. Sometimes we may be that influential parent, and at other times we may be far too permissive. Each of these styles suggests varying amounts of support and expectations for our children. The most effective parenting achieves a balance between the love and support provided and the accountability required for family expectations. Once you have identified your current style, it will be easier to determine what you want to do to intentionally move your parenting style in a direction that better meets your goals.

Stop and Reflect

Follow this link and take a quick survey to determine your dominant parenting style:
https://psychcentral.com/quizzes/parenting-style-quiz/.

What proportion of your default parenting style is characterized by influential (authoritative), permissive, uninvolved, and disciplinarian (authoritarian)? Can you think of changes you could make to gain a better balance between the support you offer and the expectations you require?

Look Inside—Identify Your Triggers and Own Them

We all have buttons. There are things our kids can do that trigger a strong emotional response in us. We may or may not act on that trigger, but we know it's there. Maybe we get mad, sad, scared, frustrated, or worried almost instantly in response to something our child does.

A mom in one of our Reset Families classes had an "aha moment" when we talked about this issue in class. She shared with us, "My daughter hates to have her hair brushed. Every morning it turns into a battle. She's in tears. I find myself yelling or saying things I don't mean. I behave in ways I am not proud of. It's an awful experience almost every single day. I have been frustrated and dread this time in the morning with my daughter."

After hearing about triggers, she was able to identify why brushing her daughter's hair was such a trigger for her. "When I was little, my mom never helped us get ready for school. My hair was always a mess, and I got made fun of at school. Now I realize that I get so frustrated over my daughter's hair because I don't want to feel like a bad mom." Once she was able to realize that her daughter's messy hair was a trigger, she could respond more appropriately, recognizing that she was transferring her past experience into the present, making things a much bigger deal than they had to be.

In *How We Love Our Kids*, Milan Yerkovich[3] writes about how our kids trigger us. "Like little coaches pointing out our weakness . . . children and teens point spotlights on the places we need to grow in our lives." When you get stuck, or find your buttons being pushed, take the time to consider the root. Why is that response there? Often, it's something unresolved from our family of origin, stress, depression, worry, low self-worth, or some past trauma. But it signals an area that we need to work on.

As a parent, we must be willing to continually look at our own challenges and allow ourselves to grow if we want our kids to have the tools to do the same. A big part of that growth is admitting and owning our mistakes with our kids. As we look at our triggers, we may discover that some have deep roots that are hard to overcome. In that case, it is best to ask for support from a trusted friend or reach out to a counselor for help working through the trigger.

Know Who Signs Your Report Card: Whose Opinion Really Counts?

One of the most challenging things about parenting can be the judgment we feel from others. Often that comes from our own family or from our partner's family. Depending on whose opinion you listen to, you are too lenient, or too strict, you are too enabling or not supportive enough, your kids are too busy or don't have enough to do.

When our son was born, we knew that we had a challenge on our hands. He knew what he wanted, and he never got it soon enough. He was incredibly determined and willful. I always said that if he had been born first, he may have been an only child. There were always people that had advice about what we needed to do, one of the most insistent being my mother. We often held different beliefs about what direction was needed to help him learn to manage his own behavior. I finally realized that I was somewhat of an expert on my son and had to listen to advice, but be confident enough to make a decision based on what would work for our family.

Being a confident parent does not come easy for most of us. But if we want to be intentional with the way we parent, we can't be blown and tossed with the waves and opinions of everyone around us. One of the best things you can do for yourself is decide whose opinion really matters. Who are the people you admire, respect, or want to be like? Who are the people you trust who care about you and your kids? Put those people on your mental committee and kick everyone else off.

We all need a few people in our life who can lead us, challenge us, question us, encourage us, teach us, and inspire us. The challenge is to allow some people to have input without letting everyone's opinion count. Surround yourself with those people who respect you, who are willing to share advice when solicited and support you on your parenting journey. Also search for authors your committee recommends and then read. Read widely. Read critically. Not everything that is published is the best advice. You can determine what resonates with you and reflects your values.

Take Time to Care for Yourself so You Can Care for Others

Laying the foundation for change in your family begins with recognizing our default parenting style and identifying and working through our triggers. As we continue to do that, we want to decide whose opinions we are going to listen to when it comes to our parenting. As we become confident of our parenting choices and are open to the input of trusted others, it is important that we create rhythms that allow us to take care of ourselves. Most of us have such full lives that it is difficult to take time for rest and reflection or to celebrate moments of peace. It is essential that we take time to figure out what fills us up or recharges us so we have something to offer our children. There are literally hundreds of self-care books available. What fills your tank may not be the same as what fills mine. Rather than following some prescription, take the time to get to know yourself and find what is most life-giving for you.

Before we move on, take a moment to think about what feeds your soul and come up with a list of practical ways you recharge in five minutes or less. Put them as reminders in your phone or computer to pop up sporadically and let you know that you need to take time to recharge. Finding time for you while raising children is no small feat. But like the instructions on the airplane, you must secure your own oxygen mask first; otherwise, despite your best intentions, you won't be helpful to those around you.

> **Stop and Reflect**
>
> Think about one self-care activity that rejuvenates you in five minutes or less. Try it now!

Lighten Up: Give Yourself a Break!

There is no such thing as a perfect parent. No matter how hard we try, we are going to mess up along the way. We will not get it right all the time. Remember to decide whose opinion really counts. Don't be too hard on yourself. Learn from your mistakes, apologize, make it right, and then forgive yourself.

There is a quote in the Bible that says, "Love each other as if your life depended on it. Love makes up for practically anything" (I Peter 4:8, MSG). If we do our best to make sure our interactions with our kids are permeated with love, when mistakes do happen there can be restoration. It is not the end of the world. Work to change unhealthy attitudes and you will make fewer mistakes.

If you are able to lighten up and give yourself a break it will help you lighten up with your kids as well. You will tend to be more in tune with your kids' emotional needs in a supportive way that will help you do away with condemnation and look for solutions rather than hanging on to unrealistic expectations.

Teach Your Child to "Take a Break"

As you get started initiating change in your family, we encourage you to notice your child's big emotions and help them express them appropriately. As a parent, you know your child well. You can often sense when they are becoming irritated or frustrated. They haven't made a poor choice yet, but you know it's only a matter of time because things are bubbling inside. That's the time to use "Take a Break."

Help them pause, identify the big emotion, and think about an appropriate response before they make a poor choice. We refer to it as a "Take a Break." This is not to be confused with "time out," so think about the best way to introduce it to your kids. You may want to describe it as "hitting the pause button." Keep your tone calm and supportive. They need to know that they are not in trouble, and taking a break is not a punishment. Rather, they take a brief break from doing what you asked them to do so they have time to refocus and make a positive choice. It gives them a chance to learn to think about their big emotions and express them appropriately. After the break, you direct them back to what you initially requested. This is not a time that lets kids off the hook as they try to avoid something they don't want to do and hope you forget. Instead, it is an important opportunity to help them develop a new self-management skill.

This tool will help your child recognize when trouble is brewing. It allows you to help your child identify signs that they are heading off track. As you practice "Take a Break," you and your child can learn to identify what happens when they feel frustrated or are ready to explode. You may ask them such questions as "What do you feel in your body? What signs do you see, such as a sigh, clenched fist, restlessness, or blurting out?"

Learning to do this early will help your child not only in difficult family situations, but also as an adult at work and in life in general. Often, our body knows we're frustrated, angry, sad, or agitated before our mind even recognizes it and well before we can articulate it. Helping your child to pay attention to the cues about their feelings in their body is a life skill that will benefit them throughout life.

"Take a Break" also helps you to avoid escalation and the need to enter into further redirection of behavior that is off target. Most importantly, it gives your child the skills to be in the driver's seat and manage those big emotions.

"Take a Break" is the first step toward self-management. It allows your child to temporarily stop doing what is expected so they can pause to consider making a better choice. You may be watching your child playing with a friend who is not sharing and notice that your child is getting frustrated and upset. Before they reach the tipping point where they lash out with angry words or hit the friend, the suggestion to "take a break" may be just what they need to figure out an appropriate solution. That brief time will help your kids redirect their own behavior by thinking about an appropriate response to the big emotions they are feeling. They may need your help to find a solution.

How Does "Take a Break" Work?

It will take some time and effort to get this off the ground. You will need to introduce this tool to your child and let them know when and how to use it. *Kids may request it when they begin to feel frustrated or angry, or parents may suggest it.* Kids should express their feelings appropriately and ask permission for a break. They may not be able to express why they need a break. They just know something's off, so that is why they need to break. But the tone and demeanor they use to request the break should be respectful. You can grant permission verbally or give them a pass card you have created. Let them know that it's not only okay, but important for them to express how they feel and know how they can manage themselves long before they lose control.

When kids become overwhelmed or frustrated and are emotionally flooded, it is very valuable for them to have an appropriate "distraction" that allows them take an emotional break so that they can come back to the situation with a new perspective. Make sure to keep "Take a Break" positive and relaxing. You may instruct them to take three deep breaths and move to their "quiet place." Your child needs to see this as a positive place, with something relaxing to do—music or a stress ball, but not with so many toys that they forget the purpose of the time.

Keep it structured: the break should be no more than two to five minutes. Make sure as you are introducing this concept the kids know this is a brief chance to pause. If they are getting overwhelmed and frustrated with homework for example, it's okay to step away for a few minutes, jump up and down, clear their head, or listen to a song. But they will need to return quickly. It is a short break, a pause. *They must come back and engage using a more appropriate response to the situation.* Do not allow this to become a "divert and forget" strategy. You may want to give them a timer that will remind them when the break is over.

If you begin to help your child with these skills, you are taking the first step toward creating an empowering environment for your family. I don't know about you, but so much of my bad behavior happens when I am feeling big emotions. Feeling frustrated, overwhelmed, stressed, angry, or tired. This is probably true for our kids as well. If we can help kids recognize their feelings, learn to label those feelings, and then problem-solve and reengage, we can help them avoid many of the behavior choices that lead to undesired consequences.

Though most of us pick up parenting books to try and figure out how to shape our child's behavior, it turns out that a big part, maybe the biggest part, of changing our family dynamics is about tuning in and understanding ourselves. As we begin to understand more about our wiring, our defaults, and how we currently react to our kids, we can make new and intentional choices. As we gain skills and deeper understanding, we acquire new tools, and then we can begin using those tools to mold and shape our family environment, which is a big part of what will shape our children.

RESET FAMILIES

Putting Reset Families into Practice in Five Minutes or Less

1. Talk with your kids about change. Encourage each family member to identify and share one small thing they would like to see change this week.

2. Tune into your child starting with the positive
   - Think about one of your child's greatest strengths and tell them about it.
   - Start to notice and complement positive behavior choices.
   - Have your child take the *Love Language Inventory*—available at https://www.5lovelanguages.com/profile/children/.
3. Notice your child's triggers. Practice identifying the underlying feelings and encourage them to "Take a break." This will work for you too!

Remember:

- Kids may request it when they begin to feel frustrated or angry or overly excitable, or parents may suggest it. Help them identify their feelings.
- Keep it structured: The break should be no more than two to five minutes.
- They must come back and engage using an appropriate response to the situation.

Further Resources, Page 173

CHAPTER 2

Creating a Shared Family Vision

In the last chapter, we suggested that the change begins with you. Strong and meaningful connections with your child begin by being aware of your default parenting style and the obstacles that stand in the way of changing your approach from reactive to intentional parenting. Intentionality puts you on your way to building a strong, connected family culture. Intentionally tuning in to your child's emotions before they erupt into poor behavior choices will help you build the family that you have often hoped and dreamed of.

The best place to start is by working to strengthen your family relationships. As kids see your commitment to building a strong family system that includes them, they are likely to believe that their hope may also become a reality. It will be easier for each of you to commit to change if you have a clear idea of what you are working toward. Change is hard. It's hard because it means learning new patterns of behavior. It's hard because what we've always done is familiar, and even if it's not great, at least it's predictable. It's hard because some of us just don't like change. But if we always do what we've always done, nothing will change. Strengthening our family connections will require change. But change to what?

It's easy to identify what we don't want our family to be like. Many of us have a list of "I'll never." And unfortunately, too many of us have examples of family systems that were damaging. Knowing what we don't want is part of the process, but having a vision for our family is about more than just what we don't want. Can you imagine going into a restaurant and telling the wait staff just what you don't want? "I don't want any tomatoes please." "I don't want soda," "I don't want crispy chicken." And then the waiter walks away, trying to figure out what to ask the kitchen to make for you. You won't get any of the things you specifically didn't want, but will it be what you hoped for? Probably not.

Many of us develop our vision for our family, beginning with the negative. Instead of pointing toward what we want, we point out what's wrong. It is much harder to get a picture of what we want, but that is the best place to begin to initiate change. With that picture clearly in mind, you have the motivation and roadmap to create a family culture where each person is valued, listened to, and has something to contribute. A clear shared vision makes it easier to see how you can experience growth yourself and how you can support your children in gaining the skills they need to be successful adults.

In reality, you will begin to intentionally set defaults for your child that will follow them into adulthood. The foundations you lay for your children provide the infrastructure on which they build their lives. If you are intentional you will be able to create defaults that are healthy and set your child up for success.

As a parent, it's impossible to get it all right. Even with the best intentions and a fabulous tool belt, we're going to make mistakes. There is lots of margin for error. We don't have to be perfect. But the more we become aware of the foundation we are laying, and the more intentional we are about helping our children develop their natural default responses to pressures life brings, the stronger their foundation will be.

We have often talked with parents who have expressed regret that they did not have a healthy model of parenting. One that prepared them with the skills they needed to be successful adults, not to mention the skills to parent their kids. Some feel that the damage done by their past experiences leaves them with little hope. Recent research in brain science has given us new understanding and hope about the possibility of repairing and changing some of that damage to help us move toward more healthy relationships with our family.

Whether your family of origin disappointed you, or you're disappointed in the foundation you have laid for your own kids so far, don't lose hope. You are not stuck. The past affects the future, but it does not have to determine it. Understanding a bit about your child's brain development will help you get started setting positive defaults for your kids.

What Does Brain Science Have to Do with Parenting?

Children are born with a well-developed lower part of the brain including the brainstem and the limbic region that is responsible for the child's most fundamental neural and mental activities. This area controls the basic functions like breathing, regulation of their sleep and wake cycles, eating, and digestion. It is also the part of the brain that causes a young child to bite or hit when they don't get what they want. Those of us who have young children are fully aware of how well-developed this area of the brain is in even the youngest.

However, the upper part of the brain or the cerebral cortex that is responsible for more sophisticated and complex thinking and behavior is underdeveloped at birth. In fact, it is growing and developing throughout childhood and adolescence. When you are parenting, it never seems to be developing fast enough. If you've ever thought, *when will she learn?* you know what I'm talking about. The cerebral cortex is responsible for a variety of thinking, emotional, and relational skills that are essential for our children to experience meaningful and balanced lives as adults.

Throughout childhood the brain is under construction, creating the structures and connections in the brain that are necessary for making decisions, regulating those big emotions, the ability to have empathy, to be flexible and adapt to new situations. As their brains develop, they are able to have insight into who they are and how they behave. As the child approaches adolescence, the brain begins to go through a remodeling process, adjusting and changing the structures that were created during childhood.

So what does this all mean for parenting? It means that we can be doing a great job helping our child to manage their behavior, make wise decisions, and display the ability to manage their emotions but the growth we see will likely not be as consistent as we were hoping for. We have to remember that their brain is changing and developing and that seldom happens in the predictable manner we would like. This means that we are going to have to be sensitive and adjust our expectations occasionally to match the developmental level of our child. It also means that at times we will have to operate as our child's brain by setting clear expectations and helping them to know what is acceptable and what is not. And it means that our consistency and predictability is so important. Their brain is constantly taking in information. We want to be intentional about sending the signals that help them grow.

During this ongoing period of brain development, we will need to help our children make decisions that they are not capable of making on their own yet. Throughout Reset Families, we will give you suggestions and activities that will help you guide your child through this process to acquire emotional and relational skills to live meaningful and productive lives both as children and adults.

There may be times as our kids are growing up where it seems that, out of the blue, they behave in a way that is frightening to us. Or for some parents, life has exposed our child to a very traumatic experience, and their behavior may lead us to believe that our lack of support and guidance has led to a situation that is not easily remedied. It may not be easily repaired, but recent brain research offers parents a lot of hope. Keep in mind that what research has identified as neuroplasticity means that our brain is more malleable than we used to think. This has big implications for all parents but especially for those who believe that there is little hope of change in a situation that is overwhelming and often frightening for them.

According to one researcher, Daniel Siegel,[4] one of the key lessons of modern neuroscience is that the power to direct our attention has within it the power to shape our brain's firing patterns . . . and to shape the architecture of the brain itself. This suggests that damaged connections or structures can be repaired so that more beneficial patterns may be created in our child's brain. Siegel suggests that the repair is most likely to happen when the parent has a strong emotional connection with the child. He says that connecting with children emotionally is the beginning of effective discipline. This emotional connection with the child or the way the parent notices the child may facilitate the repair or the rewiring process in the brain.

To sum it all up, this paints a clear picture of hope for us as parents. We can make positive changes in our families and help rewire patterns in our own brains or in our child's brain so that we can enjoy emotional connection that is the foundation for effective parenting and behavior management.

> **Stop and Reflect**
>
> Effective parenting begins with strong emotional connections. Reflect on an event with your child that ended with increased connection between you. Go and tell them how important that event was and let them know how proud you are of the way they worked with you to strengthen the connection.

The goal is to connect with kids emotionally so that they are able to learn how to control their own behavior, identify and express their feelings appropriately, and understand the impact of their behavior choices on others. So with that in mind, let's go back to the idea of setting defaults for our kids. When we consistently reinforce expectations, we are supporting the brain development that helps the child gain impulse control. The connection and reinforcement of expectations actually help the brain rewire new connections.

The good news is that you *can* change your child's defaults. That allows you to compensate for the challenging times that may have damaged relationships and help the brain rewire healthy pathways. When we realize the magnitude of the actual impact that repeated experiences can bring, it underscores the importance of being intentional about the way we interact with our children and support them in gaining skills as they grow and develop. That is the pathway for setting our child's defaults.

Jim Taylor,[5] a child psychologist, tells us that children automatically select child defaults if they do not have intentional help to deliberately choose another option. Over time, these defaults become reflexive responses to experiences they have. Eventually these become their first thoughts, emotions, decisions, and actions to virtually any situation or choice. Healthy defaults don't just happen. You intentionally "install" these choices to help your child make healthy choices over more attractive but potentially harmful alternatives.

That is exactly what you are doing as you practice recognizing big emotions and encourage your kids to take a break by pausing to think about how they could respond appropriately. You are in the process of installing healthy default choices for your child. As we continue to unpack the Reset Families model, you will find even more tools that will help your respond consistently in ways that can create pathways to positive default responses.

You can create a family culture that values relationships and learn to use this system piece by piece. Then as you spend time supporting your family in implementing change, you're going to learn how to help your kids manage their behavior, alleviate power struggles with them and hopefully be experiencing a family life that has less frustration.

As we mentioned in the beginning of this chapter, setting positive defaults for our kids and ourselves is much easier when we have taken the time to create a shared family vision. What are the hopes and dreams and what are we committed to building toward as a family? In order to begin this discussion as a family, we have a quick exercise for you to complete with your kids.

Activity

Setting the Stage for a Shared Family Vision

Supplies
- A portion of twenty to thirty Legos for each family member.
- One small box or bag used to conceal a small Lego creation.

Preparation: In secret, build a simple Lego structure and hide it in a box, bag, or even under a bowl.

Instruction: Bring your family together for this simple activity and conversation. Hold up a box that is concealing your own simple Lego creation, and give these instructions:

"Inside this box is something that I have built out of Legos. Please use the bricks on your table, to create an object that looks exactly like mine. You have two minutes."

Your family is likely to ask to see your creation. Let them know that the challenge is to build it without seeing. If they get very agitated, give them a clue (something like "I used less those twenty bricks." If they are still upset, encourage them to have fun, humor you, etc. and assure them it will be over soon.

When two minutes is up, ask: Why was that so difficult? (Get feedback.)

Building with Legos is pretty easy. After all, it's a kid's toy. And the creation I made wasn't complicated at all, so that was easy too. But the thing that made this task almost impossible is that you had no idea what you were trying to create or why I asked you to do the exercise.

Following this activity with your kids is a great time to work together as a family and begin to develop your shared family vision. We will give you some specific instructions at the end of the chapter. But before you skip to the end, let's dive a little deeper into what we mean when we talk about a family vision. The challenge you will discover with the Lego exercise is that it is nearly impossible to build something, no matter how simple, if you don't know what you are building. Often, that's the challenge when it comes to creating our family culture. We know what we don't want, but we have no idea what we are trying to create instead. If you want to have success recreating or strengthening your family culture, it needs to begin by defining what you are building toward. What are you trying to accomplish? And how are you going to do that together as a family? You will spend years building your family. Every day that passes you are laying another brick. But if you don't have an image in mind of what you're trying to create, your results will be left to chance.

One of our kids came home from preschool one day with the saying, "You get what you get, and you don't throw a fit." While this may be true when it comes to snack time at preschool, it does not have to be true when it comes to our families. As parents, we have incredible influence over the outcomes for our kids. As we work to create a shared family vision, we can shape a family culture that provides the best opportunity for our kids to flourish as adults.

Whether we are conscious of our values or not, our behavior indicates what is important to us. Clarifying our values and spending time thinking about hopes and dreams defines what we're trying to build together. It prepares us to imagine what behaviors and choices we might make as a family to reach those goals together. Here are some of the perks of creating a shared family vision you might experience:

Increase in Family Bonding

When you clarify hopes and dreams, it brings your family together on the same page and strengthens bonds. By working together, you send the message that you are a team. You are all working on a shared goal. By including your kids in the process, you have communicated that they have value and have an important role to play in the family. When they have the opportunity to contribute, they realize their contributions to the family make a difference.

Children are more likely to buy in when you begin to implement the changes that are needed in order to reach your goals when they have been included in the goal setting. No matter what the vision for your family, it is safe to say you can't accomplish the goal without time together. Time is a precious commodity, so working on this project clearly communicates that you value spending time together. As family connection is supported in this way, you are deepening family relationships—the basis for all effective discipline.

Identifies Strengths to Build On

Your family benefits from several things you do exceptionally well. Depending on your season of life, you may or may not feel like that's true, but it is. Another benefit of clarifying a shared family vision is that, it's easier to identify the things you're doing well, in addition to the areas you may want to work on. Please don't skip over the "areas we're doing well." For many, it's easy to skip directly to problem-solving what's not working. But you want to be able to identify the positive and make sure you start by celebrating what is going well in your family.

The Search Institute has developed the Family Asset Framework[6] out of their research to identify key qualities that help all types of families to be strong. They found that kids who have these assets in their families do better in life. The framework contains five major assets including: Nurturing relationships, establishing routines, maintaining expectations, adapting to challenges, and connecting to community.

What may come as a surprise is that many of the Family Assets on the list are not spectacular feats of superhuman parenting fame. Simple patterns of connecting, listening, and sharing life together set your child up for success. You're probably already doing some, or maybe even many of them. Of the ones you're not doing, there may be a few you could start doing with just a simple tweak. It is easy to look at these lists and get overwhelmed by the seeming endless list of "should." Reject the tendency to look at these lists from that perspective.

We mention the assets because we want you to focus on your family's strengths. So instead of feeling overwhelmed about what you're not doing, we encourage you to look for the things that you are already doing and celebrate them. Identifying strengths helps you to guard against focusing just on the negative, or what needs to change. It helps you celebrate the present even though it is not exactly what you hope it will be one day.

> **Stop and Reflect**
>
> Take some time right now to celebrate the temporary—look at the family asset sheet and work with your kids to identify one that you are already doing in your family.
>
> The link to the Family Asset Framework is buried but well worth the effort to search
>
> https://www.search-institute.org/wp-content/uploads/2018/02/Family_Assets_Framework.pdf

Provides an Assessment Tool

Clarifying your shared family vision also provides an assessment tool. Once you have a clear picture of where you are headed as a family, identifying the values and goals you will pursue, you have a way to measure progress. This shared family vision provides a yardstick to assess where you are in the process of moving toward your goals.

You can't measure success until you know what success looks like. If you assess and find that you are falling short of your goal, it may alert you to the need for additional tools essential to accomplish your dreams. It lets you know when it is time to reach out for help.

Provides a Foundation for Identifying and Clarifying Your Expectations

How do you go about agreeing on behavior expectations if you don't know what you're trying to build together and where you are headed? Once you have clearly defined goals, it is much easier to imagine how you need to behave in order to consistently work toward that goal. Once kids have been invited to participate in crafting the family vision, they are more likely to be involved in a discussion of the types of behaviors that will help each member of the family move toward their goals.

Without a clear goal, expectations may change depending on the emotion of the moment. The danger of failing to have a shared family vision accompanied by clear expectations is that we run the risk of falling back into our default parenting style, and our kids choose default behaviors that may not help them reach their goals.

Provides a Pattern for Consistency, Safety, and Boundaries

When you have clearly defined your shared family vision, you have created a pattern for consistency. Your family vision allows you to set clear expectations based on your goals that help you create structure, safety, and boundaries for your family. Your kids are no longer trying to guess if you're going to make them do their homework "today" or give in. In addition, you no longer have to make up answers on the spot when your kids ask "why." The shared vision provides the framework on which decisions are made. Then the reason behind each decision is more evident and easier to explain.

This doesn't mean that you will never have to revisit the vision to clarify the expectations, but it sets up the framework that is easy to revisit and update during various seasons of life and developmental stages of your children. The vision makes it easier to gather the family together and talk about how things are working. With the pattern in place, it is easy to go back and make necessary tweaks.

But What about Broken Dreams?

I'm sure some of you are sitting there thinking, *Yeah, yeah, yeah . . . I used to have hopes and dreams, but frankly, life has killed the dreams I dreamed.* I think that is true for most of us to some degree. So the thought of trying once again to identify hopes and dreams seems like it might be an exercise in frustration. However, we would challenge you to consider the importance of learning how to "Begin again." On your journey toward your shared family vision, there will be roadblocks and setbacks along the way. By including the topic of disappointment in your conversation of hopes and dreams, you prepare your family to be resilient when the setbacks come.

When you think of broken dreams, it is important to think about the range of disappointments that you experience, from being frustrated because your picnic got rained out to a pending divorce. So don't get hung up thinking that just the "big" broken dreams matter . . . In a family discussion, encourage your kids to talk about disappointing times they have had when the family has tried something new no matter how small they seem to you. It will be important to create an environment where each family member can share openly. With everyone's concerns on the table, you can discuss ways work together and imagine what you would like to see instead. Then you are ready to figure out the steps you could take to work toward your goal.

Some of you reading this book may have experienced life-shattering disappointments. If this is true for your family, be prepared to talk about devastating events. Think about what needs to be discussed with your children based on their age and developmental level. It may be wise not to include younger siblings in the discussion who were not directly impacted by the experience. With older kids you may want to frame the conversation by listening to a song. One that we have found helpful is "Tell Your Heart to Beat Again"[7] and may be found with this link: (https://www.youtube.com/watch?v=azYK8I2uoog).

Consider preparing for a conversation about challenging times by thinking about disappointments you experienced as a child and how you have recovered from them. How is it best to process so that at the end of your conversation you are all able to come to a place of hope, rather than despair? When you have thought it through, a great way to start an initial conversation or follow up conversations at times of disappointment is by being authentic and open with your kids, validating past experiences and apologizing for past challenges. Let them know you want to work together to plan a path forward. Kids need to know that they can bring hopes and dreams alive again and figure out the next step to take to build forward together.

By experiencing failure together, and gathering the strength to start again, we let our kids know that failure does not have to defeat us. I love the reminder that "You win some, you learn some." As a family, you can learn from your failures as well as successes. So be prepared to have this conversation more than once with your family. Building toward your dreams takes constant realignment. Hopes are easily dashed and disappointment and discouragement set in. As a family we must develop a response to address broken dreams so that our experiences do not end up turning the dreams we have into sources of shame and hopelessness.

If you're not ready to lead this conversation because you are feeling hopeless, we encourage you to reach out for help. Many communities have local counseling services, some organizations have free phone consultations, perhaps a mentor or a friend can walk with you, many churches offer conversations with clergy and counselors. Don't face your pain alone.

Tools for Defining Your Family Vision

Clarifying your family vision can be a daunting task. After all, how do you even begin to sort through all the possible aspirations in life to settle on the ones that are most important to you? This looks different depending on the age of your children. For those of you with very young children, as parents you will do most of this work. However, with elementary age kids you can involve them in the process. The best way to think about this project is to see it as an ongoing document that will be revisited and revised as the seasons of life change. Some people like to revisit their shared family vision each year.

In order to help you begin this process, we've broken life into four major categories: social, emotional, physical, and spiritual. What does it look like for your family to be socially, emotionally, physically, and spiritually healthy? We have posed several questions to help you think about and discuss each of these four areas. Each of these categories could occupy several chapters, but we just want you to get started discussing these ideas with your kids as a way to formalize your shared family vision.

The Social Area of Life

The social area of life is all about relationships. When you think about your hopes and dreams, what do you hope relationships within your family look like? Your hopes, goals, and ideals around the relationship between parents, between parents and children, and between siblings are all worth exploring.

In addition, what significant relationships do you hope to create or maintain outside the household? What would you like your connection to extended family to be like? Some people value time spent with extended family and want to make grandparent relationships or cousin connection priorities in their lives. Others may have come from broken family systems and will choose to create space between themselves and their extended family.

Beyond your family, do you have important relationships with friends and social groups? Do you have hopes and dreams about the priority these relationships hold for your family? If so, you may want to write that down. As you explore the social area of life, ask yourself and your kids how your relationships add to your life. This is a great time to think about how you choose your friends, or the people you spend time with. How do you add to others' lives through relationship? How are you involved in giving back in the world around you? How are you building relationships with others in your community who may not be as fortunate as you are? What are your family values around building relationships with people of diverse cultural or socioeconomic backgrounds? All these questions will help you decide together as a family what you want the social area of life to look like.

Without taking the time to think about your relationships both inside the family and beyond, it is easy to get out of balance expending too much time and effort on relationships that have little meaning in the long run. We may spend time working on our most meaningful relationships in ways that harm our emotional connections rather than making them stronger. We may focus too much energy

SHARED FAMILY VISION

on the negative and not pay enough attention to the positive aspects of our most valued relationships.

The Emotional Area of Life

The emotional area of life is all about our feelings. There are two ends of the spectrum when it comes to feelings. There are those who are practically a slave to their feelings, being blown and tossed in every direction. Then there are those who deny they have feelings or do their best to avoid or dismiss them at all costs. Most of us are somewhere in between. Wherever you find yourself on the spectrum, most admit that feelings are an important part of life. On any given day, especially in a home with children, you will navigate feelings both positive and challenging. They are unavoidable. Understanding the importance of feelings and thinking through the way you want to navigate feelings in your family can have a huge impact on your family.

In *Raising an Emotionally Intelligent Child: The Heart of Parenting, Gottman*[8] it indicates that the way parents respond to their child's feelings can impact every aspect of the child's development. There is a correlation between a parent's ability to respond to their child's big emotions and walk them through them and the child's health and well-being as an adult. Gottman found that if parents will recognize emotions as an opportunity to connect and help their kids identify and express their feelings *before* jumping to problem-solving, kids are healthier. The emotional area of life matters too much to take for granted.

When it comes to your family vision, how are feelings expressed and acknowledged? How do family members feel about themselves? Obviously, no exercise or family-values chart can determine how someone feels about himself. But by identifying what we want people to know about their value, worth, and importance, we are able to focus energy on reminding them of their value. And we are more likely to intervene when the family environment threatens that goal.

In our house, we frequently talk about how the world, especially the middle-school world, is a tough place. We want our home to be a sanctuary from all the put-downs, trash talk, belittling, and criticism that kids so often experience outside the home. Because this is our value, we are relentless about helping our kids encourage or edify each other, rather than being critical. As parents, we keep ourselves in check when we are tempted to point out what's wrong, more often than we celebrate what's right.

We are able to tune in to the emotional aspect of life, because we have identified our values around that part of life of life. Here are some additional questions that will help you identify your values in this area: What is the expectation for the ways you handle other people's feelings? What limits do you put in place to safeguard and care for emotional health? Do you minimize or deny the need to care for yourself and your children emotionally? Have you found a way to embrace your emotional health and take the time necessary to find a long-term plan to promote emotional health for your entire family?

As you begin to identify your values, you may find you have some messes to clean up. You may have patterns of behavior, interaction, or language that move you further from your goals rather than closer to them. In that case, confessing your shortcomings and being willing to be accountable when you slip up in the future is a great way to begin to change your family culture.

When feelings are expressed and validated, it is much easier to find ways to support each other in emotionally healthy ways. It is very important that we take time to listen and hear what our kids are saying and to encourage them to express their feeling, with an emphasis on appropriateness. One of the quickest ways to undermine your emotional connection with your child or partner is to tell them that they "shouldn't feel that way." Our challenge is not to deny the feelings they have, but to help them express them in a manner that is productive. How they feel matters, but that will be lost if we fail to help them express their feelings in a manner that they can be heard and received.

SHARED FAMILY VISION

The Physical Area of Life

The physical area of life is all about our bodies. We only get one of them, and they come in all different shapes, sizes, and ability levels. In your family, what value is placed on physical health and nutrition? It is easy to go to extremes with both health and nutrition. Challenge your kids to think about balance. How are you intentional about resting? Depending on your wiring, you may see rest as laziness rather than a necessary form of rejuvenating your body and mind. Our bodies thrive on healthy rhythms around rest and activity. Another question worth exploring is how often will you exercise? Or what priority does exercise take? Like all of us, our kids are probably more likely to engage in exercise if it is fun. What are the ways you like to be active both individually and together?

We live in a culture that is very concerned about body image, so the messages we send need to be well thought out. Are you preoccupied with your appearance? Do you value or devalue people based on their looks? Is exercise about how you look or about your health? Perhaps it's both. This is a great opportunity to help the kids express their thoughts and feelings about their bodies and to make certain that it is safe for them to express thoughts without fear of condemnation or judgment. If they are vulnerable about their feelings, it is critical others in the family do not minimize or make fun of their thoughts. Make certain that body shaming is not tolerated in any form.

The physical area of life is also about the safety of our physical body. What boundaries will do we put in place to safeguard the physical health of our families? When our kids are very young, we may use baby gates to keep them from tumbling down the stairs. We teach them to hold our hands and eventually look both ways before crossing the street. As they grow, we probably encourage the use of safety gear like bike helmets. The privilege of driving a car likely comes with the expectations that our kids will follow traffic laws put in place for their safety, like stopping at red lights and sticking to the speed limit.

More than coming up with a list of rules for everything, we want to express our values around our bodies. When my kids ask for a treat after school, they may hear our values around food expressed in my response. Rather than a simple "yes" or "no" as an option, the question is an opportunity to express values. A response like "treats are fun, but right now, I think your body needs some protein. After your body has what it needs, then maybe you can have a little treat." The value expressed is that we want to give our body what it needs, and sometimes a little of what it might want too.

When a preschooler refuses to get in her car seat, she may hear a reflection of values: "I want you to be happy, but in order for that to happen, we have to keep you safe." One of our expressed family values is that safety is a team endeavor. I have a role to play in keeping my kids safe, and they have a role to play too. As they get older, more of the responsibility for their safety shifts from me, to them. Because of our team values around safety, this is a natural progression. As our children grow, the need to have clearly expressed and hopefully agreed upon values becomes increasingly important.

It's natural for children to resist arbitrary rules as they seek to differentiate themselves from their parents. But if we take the time to create shared family values, we've laid a great foundation for kids to make their own choices based on their own values. Hopefully values we've helped them form over hundreds of little interactions along the way.

What about the use of drugs? Like it or not, culture is sending messages to our kids about values and norms around these important physical aspects of life. Finding ways to create our own family messages on these important topics matters. Sitting our kids down for "the talk" once or twice isn't going to come close to helping them mold and shape their values. Open communication and encouraging simple reflections to cultural messages can help our children form their own healthy values. How do you help your kids make good decisions about drugs and alcohol? Are they able to say no and still keep their friends? It is never too early to clarify the family position on the use of drugs and alcohol both for those who are old enough to use and those who are not.

It is helpful in such discussions to respond to the kids' questions from a positive perspective, rather than one of denial. Here's what I mean by that: Children will often ask, can I drink alcohol; the answer may be "yes, when…" rather than "no". When they are old enough to legally drink, they will have to decide if and how they wish to drink alcohol. The discussions you have long before that time are going to help them to have the tools to make responsible decisions. If you have a strong family position on no use of alcohol, it will be helpful to discuss the reasons with the children, such as a family history of alcoholism, personal or religious belief. Depriving your children without discussion often creates an intensified desire to try what is forbidden.

Your example here is incredibly powerful, so make certain that you are responsible in your use of alcohol and drugs, whether prescription or, in some states, recreational. Your words will have little value if your actions carry a different message.

Also related to the physical part of life are your hopes and dreams regarding the sexual part of their lives. What you hope for them is important, but they need to know the whys of your position. Their own ideas around sexuality are far more powerful and influential than your own ideas. So teaching them how to think about these issues will have greater potential than telling them what to think. If you want them to abstain from or put off sexual relationships, discuss why you believe that is important. As you state your position, you are teaching them how to think about these decisions rather than simply saying no. Sex is being talked about all the time, on television, in music, and definitely in the hallways of middle schools and high schools across the country. So equip your kids with the information to make informed decisions.

As with so many issues, identifying the good you want for your child in the area of sexuality is just as important as communicating the perils you want them to avoid. When we are young, it is natural to feel invincible. It is hard for any teenager to believe that pregnancy, STDs, or someone sharing a sexually explicit text would really happen to them. Remember, setting the tone around family values actually starts when our kids are young. Values around physical affection can be shaped well before the conversation turns to sex. We may encourage our kids to use their voice if someone makes them feel uncomfortable. We may teach them to always honor someone's request when they don't want you to be in their personal space. These kinds of conversations lay the foundation for talking about sexuality in the preteen years.

The Spiritual Aspect of Life

The spiritual aspect of life is all about our most deeply held values. It is easy to just assume that our kids know what values we believe are important. As a result, we often fail to discuss spiritual values with them and help them identify the framework for our values. As you think about a shared family vision for the spiritual aspect of life, consider these questions: Where do you derive your most deeply held values? How do you look beyond yourselves and reach for help? Where do you find hope when life feels hopeless? Where do we look for answers to the toughest questions? What is your connection to the natural world and how does that relate to the spiritual part of life? What does spiritual health look like for your family? What customs, practices, or traditions are in place to deepen your sense of spiritual connection?

The spiritual part of life is about more than rules. Religion can often default to a set of rules. It is not that rules are bad, but they can be harmful when applied without relationship. Rules, when not connected to the bigger picture or established in the context of relationship, often lead to rebellion. Very few people like to be told what to do especially without any sense of why the guidelines or rules are in place. A legalistic set of rules rarely leads to hope, strength, or endurance, all of which are resources we hope our children can draw from the spiritual part of life.

Legalistic practices can lead to people trying to prove their worth or earn love by following a set of rules. Remember that an important part of exposing your children to a source of spiritual strength is an open and trusting relationship where it is safe to explore belief as well as doubts that arise. When we can point our children toward a source of hope and strength, within an environment where they are empowered to explore their own beliefs, it can be a deep well they can draw from throughout their lives.

Depending on how you view spirituality, be sure to be intentional about sharing your journey with your children when age-appropriate. Have you found hope in an ancient text or spiritual practice? Let your kids see you engaging in the practice or reading the text. Have you experienced an answer to prayer? Share it with your kids. Is there a tradition that helps you feel connected to something bigger than the physical world? Invite them to be a part of it. Are there days of significance for you? Make them special for your kids too. Often, we keep our spiritual world private, but then when our children face their own questions about the deeper things in life, they are left feeling untethered, needing to start from scratch to fill in their own blanks. One of the best gifts we can offer our children is a connection to a source of hope, strength, and purpose beyond what is immediately obvious. In the absence of this connection, it can be easy to be weighed down by fear of the future, stress for today, and shame about our past. Taking the time to explore your values around the spiritual part of life and sharing those values with your kids can be an important part of creating your family culture.

Activity

You don't have to finish reading the book to do this project. To get you started, we suggest a family project you can do together in one evening. Be sure to provide a special treat to help boost enthusiastic participation. For really resistant family members, you may think about rewarding contribution with a special treat. For example, a single M&M, Skittle, Smartie, or Starburst for each thought shared. Or make several bite-sized treat options and allow them to choose a bite for their contributions in each category.

As a family, talk about your hopes and dreams for the future. As the leader, you can help inspire thinking by asking some of the questions contained in the sections above. After brainstorming your thoughts, choose a way to visually represent your family hopes and dreams. Refer to Sheet page 175.

Some families like to create a poem or poster. Others like to represent their values through a magazine collage or even using photographs of their own family engaging in the practices they value. Some families choose to make hopes-and-dreams jars, which contain cards or tokens representing their hopes and dreams. One parent even included glue and white out to remind them that there may be broken promises that need to be mended and mistakes that need to be corrected. They keep the jar in the middle of their table and draw one card at random each night as a reminder of their values. Others choose to use words that represent their hopes and dreams and create a word college.

Keep them simple, using resources you may have at home. Allow your children to contribute their ideas to the project. Examples of family vision projects may be found at www.resetfamilies.org.

SHARED FAMILY VISION

Putting Reset Families into Practice in Five Minutes or Less

1. Continue to notice the positive behavior choices your children are making and give them concrete praise for those choices.
   - Make it authentic and specific, validating their hard work and the values their choice demonstrates.
   - For example: "I'm proud of the way you worked out the problem with your brother all by yourself" or "Wow! Thanks for cleaning your room. You did a great job organizing your toys."
2. Continue to recognize your child's big emotions, helping them identify their feelings. Encourage them to "take a break" so they are able to express them appropriately.
3. Work with your kids to create a representation of your shared family vision.
   - Consider the social, emotional, physical, and spiritual aspects of life.
   - Refer to the Family Assets Sheet for ideas about what quality family looks like.
   - Use "Clarifying Hopes and Dreams" Sheet to gather ideas
   - Talk to friends or family who have family relationships you respect.
   - Make sure each family member has a voice in the final project.

> "There are a million no's that stand in the way of our dreams . . . no time . . . no chance. But we only need one yes. Dreams don't come true; they are made true."
> —Russell Wilson, Quarterback, Seattle Seahawks

Further Resources, Page 175

CHAPTER 3

Strengthening Family Connections

In the first two chapters, we talk about ways to create and sustain a family culture that nurtures each member. As we become leaders in the family, and then empower our kids to help make change possible, we are setting a tone for a family that learns and grows together.

In order to accomplish any of this, we have to be a team. Our family relationships will be an important key to success. When we start talking about strengthening family connections, it doesn't take long to figure out that in order to do that, we have to spend time together. I know what some of you might be thinking: *Our life is so incredibly busy going in all directions for sports leagues, dance lessons, school activities, work obligations, cooking, cleaning, and . . . the list is endless. We can hardly get five minutes together in the same room.*

On your way to work some day or in one of your quiet moments take the time to listen to the Harry Chapin song "Cat's in the Cradle."[9] The song takes you on the journey of a father with young kids at home. While he is young, the child makes bids for his dad's attention, but the dad is always too busy with work and life. As the song progresses, the kid grows and becomes busy. Now, when the dad wants to spend time with the son, the son does not have time for the father. It's a tragic story, really, about two people who pass each other and miss the opportunity to connect. In the end, both are disappointed in the relationship they have. The song suggests that real relationship involves sacrificing some "good" things in order to say "yes" to the most important things like investing time with those we love.

> **Stop and Reflect**
>
> Using the song as inspiration, think about your current family dynamics. Do you have time for the relationships that matter most to you? How often do your kids' bids for connection get ignored? We can't stop what we're doing every time our kids want to connect, but do we have a rhythm for ensuring the responsibilities of life don't lead to a missed connection? If you have older kids, how are their schedules working for family connection? How have you modeled the priority of time spent with family? Take a moment to jot down a few ideas of things you can do to strengthen your family connections so you avoid the same outcome of the father and son in "Cats in the Cradle."

Before we jump into some of the ways that we can intentionally strengthen family connections, let's review what we know about creating a family culture where parents and kids can grow together. Have we created a culture that encourages and supports our kids to manage their own behavior and build together toward a shared family vision?

In chapter one we recognized that change isn't easy. Being aware of both the benefits of change and the obstacles we face are great first steps to initiate change. Improving our family relationships is the goal of most parents and is the beginning of effective discipline. A system such as Reset Families is only as good as our commitment to identifying the change we need to make to taking actions that support building strong family relationships, rather than interfering with family connections.

In chapter two we encouraged you to work toward creating a shared family vision. Not one where you hand out the rules and expect the kids to obey, but an honest and open discussion about what each member of the family thinks about changes they would like to see to move toward the family they hope for. Thinking back to the Lego activity we described, we acknowledged that if we want to create change in our family, we have to know what we are trying to build. Our shared family vision, the expression of our hopes and dreams, paints the picture of where we are going. Without that we may spend years having a great desire to have a close family but experience frustration and anger, rather than the relationship we desire so much.

As you develop a shared family vision, you will want to make sure you are taking steps toward realizing that vision rather than just talking about it. The best way to start is to work on strengthening family connections. A family is a lot like a sports team. You are a group of people who will need to depend on each other for shared success, so take some time to bond together. Are there ways you can have more fun together and make your connections more intentional and meaningful?

It might seem strange that we suggest that you spend time together as a family. After all, you live in the same house and probably go to a lot of activities together. But that is exactly why it's so important to be a bit more intentional. We are a busy generation with a whole lot of distractions that can get in the way of quality time together as a family. Occupying the same physical space as your family does not necessarily equate to togetherness. If you need evidence of that, how long are your guests at your house before they ask for your Wi-Fi code or have their phones out, interacting with people who aren't even there? How often is your family sitting in the same room but each in their own virtual reality? The numbers of distractions vying for our attention are greater today than at any other time in history. Family time is no longer a given in our society.

The Importance of Spending Time Together

Spending time together is a vital element to building a strong family culture and to achieving your shared family vision. First, it demonstrates your desire and priority to spend time together. Like in most areas of life, actions speak louder than words. By those actions, you are setting defaults for your children whether you realize it or not. If you say you want to spend time together, but rarely set aside time to do it, you are sending a strong message. Have you ever had a friend who says, "We should get together," but whenever you try to arrange something they don't have time? If that happens often enough, you start to doubt their desire to spend time with you. The same is true with our kids. The only way to convince your kids that you value family time is to prioritize family time.

If you have older kids, you may think they don't want to spend time with you. This is a logical conclusion to come to since there is a good chance your teens drag their feet or roll their eyes when you suggest the idea. However, *The Journal of Youth and Adolescence*, Greenberg, Siegel and Leitsch[10] suggest that you are actually still the most important person in your teen's life. Even as your kids are stretching their wings and trying on independence, they still want to spend time with you, but they are rarely willing to admit it. Their resistance to your request for time may indicate that they want to spend time differently. The best way to discover how they want to spend time with you is by asking them.

They may enjoy having a role in planning the activities or having specific responsibilities during the time together. Sometimes, if kids are having a hard time thinking of what they would like to do, giving them choices helps. They can at least tell you what they really don't like. The important part is giving them voice in the decision of how to spend time together. I have made the mistake on both sides of this issue. There have been times I have assumed my teenage children would not want to participate in a family activity, only to discover they felt left out when we went to see Santa without them. Other times, I've tried to plan really cool family outings I'm sure they'll love only to have them engage with poor attitudes, much to my disappointment. The lesson for me was, ask for their input. Maybe not every time, but brainstorming ideas from time to time is a good way to help them feel heard and increase their willingness to participate. If you want your family to spend quality time together, even when your kids are grown, you have to begin by making it a priority now.

When you are intentional about making family time a priority, you create the opportunity for fun and sharing life together. If asked the question, "Do you want to have fun with your kids?" most parents would answer yes without hesitation. But wanting to have fun and making time for fun are two separate things. By establishing a set family time, you create space for your family to lighten up and just have some fun together. It's easy for whatever time we do get together as a family to be consumed with solving problems, so as you get started, be sure to make fun a priority in your family time. When we instituted family time in our house, the initial reaction to our invitation to family time, or a family meeting, was "uh oh." Our kids assumed someone was in trouble. That told us something. Apparently, the only time we were intentional with our family time was when something had gone wrong. So by creating a rhythm of intentional time spent together, we were able to rewrite that story for our kids. Family time, even family meetings, aren't just for solving problems. They are a great way to get to know each other better, to work together as a team, and to laugh a little more.

Spending scheduled time together also provides an opportunity to develop skills in your kids, or maybe even yourself! Family time can be a great place to develop skills that will be useful for years to come. Learning to express thoughts and communicate ideas in a group and practicing things like planning and leadership are all skills kids can gain through family meetings. We started making family meetings a priority when our kids were in elementary school. It wasn't long before our son, aged ten, announced that he wanted to create the agenda so that we could use our time better. He went to each family member to get their input for the agenda, and the quality of the meetings improved! I am not sure we would have recognized that skill had we not been intentional about our time together. It also gave us the opportunity to recognize and support his natural bent. It allowed all of us to see how much each member of the family can truly contribute to achieving our shared family vision. It was one of those unexpected outcomes.

A family culture that prioritizes spending time together makes space for fun and the opportunity to gain skills. In addition, it provides the venue for having intentional conversations that increase buy-in. When kids are invited into the discussion and allowed to be a part of the decision-making process, they are more willing to support the plan when it emerges. Some families allow members to take turns planning family times. Others assign different roles to each family member and rotate them. As we take time to identify our kids' areas of interest and skills, we can identify tasks that speak to that skill. You may invite your child to play a musical piece that they have learned at school or in private lessons. For those kids who enjoy creativity in the kitchen, you may ask them to provide a special treat. You might be surprised by what you discover as you invite their input!

Finally, spending intentional time together strengthens family bonds. Shared experiences are powerful. They make an impression on us, and we often remember them for years to come. Think back on some of your favorite family moments as a kid. Not all of us have happy memories from our childhood, but if you have memories of times together, think about what you were doing during those happy memories. We want to create lots of memories for our kids. It doesn't have to be a Disneyland moment. It can be simple things like favorite board games, road trips, or even those crazy calamities that sometimes result from our best attempts to spend time together. You may laugh for years about things that happen during family times, both the success and the epic failures. Those shared memories help bond you together.

One of my favorite memories of our kids growing up occurred during a season when we were short on discretionary money for vacations. So when our friends were taking their kids to Disneyland we decided that creativity would allow us to have an adventure. Our kids were eight and twelve when we planned a motorcycle adventure that spanned 1,100 miles largely on forest service roads. My husband and I each had small enduro motorcycles. We packed our backpacking equipment and a kid on the back of each bike and headed out on the adventure of our lives. We purchased minimal groceries along the way, hunting, fishing, and gathering our meals each day. The cost of gasoline for the trip was under fifteen dollars. We took one book along to read and spent evenings around the campfire. The family bonding that developed on that trip is still the topic of conversation today as we listen to our adult kids sharing the story with their own children. Creativity often surpasses money when it comes to time together.

Maybe you don't have motorcycles or camping gear. Your family has its own kind of fun waiting to happen. When was the last time you purposely turned off the power and "camped out" in the living room? What if you made s'mores around a campfire, even in winter? What about declaring a videogame-a-thon night in your house where you try your best to conquer the digital roadblocks you encounter? What if you put your six-year-old in charge of your Friday-night plans, from dinner to entertainment? What would they choose, and could you get the rest of the family to play along if they knew their day was coming too? What about building an elaborate blanket fort as a family and then eating dinner (or dessert) inside while playing a game, answering "Would you rather" questions, reading a book, or telling stories about your day. Eat dessert first every Saturday. Build cars out of boxes and have a "drive-in" movie night. Google *geocaching* and give it a try. Let your kids teach you something, even if you're sure you're going to fail.

The possibilities are endless, but the fun starts when you set aside time to say yes to fun. So many things vie for our time. You will need to be tenacious if you really want to make family time a priority. When your kids are young, it often works to set aside the same time each week. As our children grow, and have activities and schedules of their own, this can become more difficult. You may want to consider setting an alarm in your phone for Sunday evening or some other time that works to look at your calendars for the next week and set a time for family time. Be sure you and your kids are on the same page about the priority of family time. There may be times when other plans have to be canceled or rescheduled to make time for what is more important.

> *Stop and Reflect*
>
> What are some of the best family times you've had? What do you remember most and what was the cost of the event? What are some of the barriers you anticipate having to family times? Do you have any ideas for helping others overcome the barriers?

Intentional Conversations

While fun is a high priority for family time, we also want to invite you to have intentional conversations! Along with all the other benefits of family time, as we mentioned earlier, it also provides the opportunity to have intentional conversations with our kids. This allows us to move away from our default parenting style and become the parent we mean to be. Rather than confronting issues when we're frustrated, we can wait until we're in a better space. Rather than making all the decisions, we can include our kids and increase their level of buy-in to the solutions. Regular family conversations help lay a foundation for open dialogue. If your kids believe they'll be heard, they are more likely to come to you when problems arise.

In each chapter, we will suggest a topic that you can use in your family time together. Each topic helps create understanding of the principles that help you become a Reset Family. These discussions that you have with your children are building the framework necessary for introducing the Reset Families behavior-management system. Trust us with the pace we are taking. The work we are currently suggesting is helping you create the family culture that is most likely to help your kids become self-managers.

The intentional conversations that you have with your kids are not only important for establishing a new behavior system, but also for your health as a family. Often parents with young kids, super-busy kids, or kids who have a hard time focusing hear us suggesting family conversations and immediately think, *That will never work at my house.* But before you begin arguing in your mind that you could never have a "meeting" with your kids at their age, at least consider the importance of communicating this information to your kids at an age where they can more fully participate. Consider changing your definitions of meetings, or simply call the time together something that reflects the culture of your family.

Intentional time doesn't have to be long. Five minutes of focused time is often enough to begin an intentional conversation on a very important topic that you revisit another time. It doesn't have to happen all at once! It is easier to develop the habits and create your family culture while your kids are young. So the sooner you start, the better, even if the conversations have to be short. If you didn't or couldn't start early, just start now. It's never too late. We are going to help you adapt the conversations for the age of your children as we make suggestions for your time together.

Intentional conversations add so much to your family dynamics. First of all, they allow you to make key family decisions together. Including your kids in the decision-making process helps them see that you value them and want their input. As we have said before, you get much higher levels of buy-in by soliciting their input than when you just tell them how it's going to be. Family time provides a great opportunity to put topics on the table for discussion and allows everyone the opportunity to weigh in. This doesn't mean that everyone has an equal say, or that you can always make everyone happy. But allowing each family member to feel like they have a voice will go a long way toward them feeling part of the process.

Intentional conversations create the setting for you to clarify expectations and consequences as you get your family on board with a new commitment to behavior that meets family goals and values. If the only time we talk about expectations and consequences is after our kids have blown it, they aren't in the best place to hear the discussion. If you're frustrated, you may not be in the best place to communicate intentionally either. A family meeting provides a great setting where you remind each other of the expectations that the family has agreed to. In my experience, without reinforcement, things are often lost in the shuffle and business of life. We benefit from taking the time to reflect on the expectations so that we remember what to be looking for both to celebrate success with the kids as well as correct and clarify behavior choices that are off target. We all benefit from the redundancy that helps those expectations become woven into our lives as a family team.

In addition, intentional conversations demonstrate value by giving each person in the family voice. I know we say this over and over, but it is so important. From the time a baby lets out the first wail, they are looking for the answer to the questions "Does anyone hear me? Does anyone care? Does my voice matter?" Our response to our children answers this question for them over and over. Giving our kids voices is the difference between empowering and disempowering. It is important to note that having a voice is often confused with always getting your way. Giving our kids voice means giving them a chance to be heard. It is an opportunity to express their thoughts and feelings. Including kids in the change process by giving them voice results in them feeling valued. Intentional conversations give us the structure and opportunity to impart both voice and value as they grow and change.

Hopefully by now you see the value in establishing a family time that makes intentional conversation a priority. We have talked about fun being one of the most important elements of family time if we are going to build shared memories or even get our kids to participate. Family time is a great time for meaningful conversations where we talk about what really matters. Unfortunately, schedules that are maxed out with activities and technology not only in every room, but in every hand, means that we will have to be determined and steadfast in our pursuit.

Our daily choices and interactions create the culture of our family whether we are being intentional or not. Purposeful family time helps us to create a culture of connection that will last a lifetime. Instead, so many of us end up, by default, caught up in the swirl of life and are left with a family culture that is the result of what's left over, rather than what matters most.

If establishing a family time is not already a part of your habit, it could be challenging. You may run into all kinds of resistance, but keep pursuing time together. It is worth it. Here are some tools to help you get started!

Getting Started with Family Time

Hopefully by now, we've convinced you that establishing a family time is worthwhile. But how can you get started making this a reality in your family? As you first attempt to get this started, don't expect to be able to get it going quickly, easily, and successfully immediately. It begins with your attitude and will move forward as you are committed to trying ideas, making adjustments that fit your family and trying again.

Step One: Create the Atmosphere

1. **Make Family Time Fun!**

   Think about your values or hopes and dreams. They probably included a lot more hoping for happiness and joy than sadness and misery. Make sure your family time each week reflects that value by infusing it with fun. What is fun for every family is different. What's fun for every person is different. You may not be able to make everyone happy all the time, but you can try to include aspects that offer everyone the opportunity to have fun and enjoy the family time. This can be a quick challenge or game that you work on together, but keep it light and engaging.

   Just a caution here: when you think about making changes in your family, it is all too easy to get hung up on what is wrong. We often get intense and focused on the negative, and that gets the family time off on the wrong foot. I remember an experience we had with a foster son soon after he came to our home. We announced that we wanted to have a family meeting and he disappeared. When we went to look for him, he was under his bed in the fetal position. To him family meeting meant nothing but trouble. So make certain that as you get each family time started, begin and end with fun. Keep it light. These times should include laughter and have a lightness about them, even during the discussions of challenges.

   To get started on the right foot, use the first "planned" family time to plan something fun! Your kids may be leery of something new, much like our foster son was. They may think that *family time* is a code word for "someone's in trouble," or "time for another lecture," or "here comes bad news." Or they may just assume it will be boring because, let's face it, we adults can be boring. Dispel their fears and tensions by starting with something fun. Keep the conversation light. Practice spending time together as a family. That is going to take work but is worth the effort.

2. **Get Rid of Interruptions**

Agree ahead of time to reserve the time only for family interaction. Set aside electronics, video games, TV in the background, cell phones, and MP3 players and instead connect with each other. This may be very tough for your kids so be sure to make it worth it for the entire family. It also may be tough for you. You may need to practice ignoring your message notifications, just for a little while. Some families toss all the technology into a basket so that the temptation is removed. By setting aside distractions you are making the statement that family time is a priority and worth the effort. It's not that family time couldn't include technology, like playing a game together. Instead, the removal of technology is about encouraging everyone to be fully present, in the room, with the people they live with, just for a little while.

3. **Set Aside a Consistent Time**

By setting aside family time consistently, we emphasize the priority. Family time isn't something that happens if there is time left over. It's important, and therefore it's planned for. If you are able to set aside the same time each week, that's ideal. If kids are older, sports turnouts and work schedules may fluctuate, and your own schedule is probably full. If there are barriers to doing it on the same day and time, then just decide on the same day each week that you will put schedules together and get your family time on the calendar. For example, every Sunday, when everyone has their work schedules for the week, we can get together and set aside time for family some time during the week. Remember the saying, "Failure to plan is planning to fail." When we get out of the habit of planning family time, it doesn't take long before we've gone weeks without spending intentional time together.

4. **Be Willing to Negotiate**

If you have a family member who is really resistant to family time, be willing to negotiate or make a trade to help them decide to spend time with the family. It may not be important to them. They may have other things they'd rather be doing with their free time. However, this is a great time to explain teamwork and how each member of the family participates in something that is valuable to others. There will be a time there is something they want others to participate in that may not seem valuable to them either. Ask for their input on family activities, and be willing to reward family members for active participation in family time. There are lots of great ways to lower resistance. We've begun a list below, but you may have other ideas you can add to the list that fit for your family.

Stop and Reflect

Ideas for lowering resistance

- Think about a couple of things that might help this time seem worthwhile for a resistant child in your family.
- Here are few ideas to get you started thinking about what will work for your kids
- Serve dessert
- Ask for input on fun things to do
- Listen to things your kids indicate they want to do, and make that a part of family time
- Be creative, even silly; color outside of the lines. Maybe dessert before dinner, spraying whipped cream into their mouths from the can or other messy games.
- Give them something to look forward to. Maybe older kids can stay up later on family nights to make up for the missed "free time."

STRENGTHENING FAMILY CONNECTIONS

Step Two: Plan for Success

1. Make a Plan, and Follow the Plan for Each Family Time

Using the Family Connection Planning Guide; begin by filling in your scheduled date, time, and the budget you have for this family time. (page 178) Plan what you will have for snacks and who is responsible to get them ready. Who leads the next family time? What are the items for discussion? Take turns deciding the check-in activity and leading it. These are great opportunities to get the kids involved in an area they can shine.

2. Check-In

Use the Check-in Activity Sheet, p. 178, or Emotion Chart, p. 178 in "Further References," to give everyone an opportunity to check in. The emotion chart may work better for the younger ones. Check-in is a great way to catch up with each other and give each person the opportunity to share how they are doing in a fun, but meaningful, way. We have suggested ways in the last two chapters to help our kids handle their "big emotions." Then encourage them to identify their feelings, and give voice to those feelings in positive ways. We have also introduced the need to take a break if we are not ready to express our feeling in an appropriate manner. This would be a great time to use some quick and fun games that help your kids develop self-control: https://www.youtube.com/watch?v=H_O1brYwdSY.

Taking time each week to check in is a great chance to give each person voice and help them check themselves to see if they are ready to have fun together. They may just need a few minutes to have someone validate a hard day they had or celebrate a success!

3. Set the Ground Rules in the Beginning

Refer to the Ground Rules Sheet, page 178 in "Further References." This is a great pattern to use in deciding your own "rules" to use during family meeting time.

Talk with your kids about including everyone and making it safe for all. Have this discussion about ground rules in the beginning, so you can help keep it fun and engaging for everyone. If you hope to have good conversations where everyone contributes and everyone feels heard, you'll have to lay the foundation. Good ground rules can help you do that.

Whenever possible, it's great to get buy-in from your kids by asking them what they think the ground rules should be. You may wish to modify these ground rules for your family, add to them, or use them exactly as is. The important thing to remember is that this is a great place to start clarifying expectations, by setting them for one small part of your family interaction.

As part of our family-time resource kit, we have included the suggested ground rules for family conversations. Ground rules include:

1. Everyone gets a chance to talk.
2. One person talks at a time and doesn't get interrupted.
3. It's okay to say what you feel—use *I* statements.
4. No one has to talk.
5. Everyone has to listen.
6. No one puts anyone down.

4. Have intentional conversations:

Refer to our discussion of intentional conversations on page 60. In the chapters that follow, we will give you a suggested conversation topic for the first few meetings to get you going. Remember, your goal for the first meeting is to have a conversation about planning a fun time together.

5. Choose a family activity:

What's fun for one kid may not be fun for the next, but try to find something that most can enjoy. And if it's silly, that makes it hard not to love. You can keep family nights simple, like a family game followed by dessert and conversation. There are preschool games that are crazy enough for everyone to love like Hungry, Hungry Hippo, so if you have kids of a variety of ages, you can keep things lively that way. Or you can add to the fun. One suggestion would be to build a giant blanket fort together and then eat dinner or dessert while hanging out in your blanket fort. The cozy atmosphere provides the perfect opportunity for conversation. But don't drag it out too long, or the kids will go stir crazy, you end up in a power struggle, and family time loses its appeal!

If you have a wide range of ages, it might work better on some occasions to have family time with the school-age kids after the little ones are in bed. It is also beneficial to have a separate family time with appropriate activities based on the ages. The little ones often have more structured time with you out of necessity to keep them engaged or safe. So make sure you provide the same for the older kids.

> **Stop and Reflect:**
>
> Make a quick list of five activities that would be developmentally appropriate and fun for your entire family. If you are having trouble, get together with a few friends and share ideas. There are several websites such as Pinterest that have activities to keep you busy for several years to come.

6. Assign tasks:

Refer to the Family Connection Planning Guide, p. 178 in appendix.

What do you need to do to get ready for the next meeting and who does what? Assign the tasks to all who are able to contribute. If you have young children, think of some small way they can help get ready for the time together. Older kids may want to make their favorite dish or snack or help get the gear into the car. Be creative, and allow the kids to make suggestions and choose the task they wish to do. We found that it was helpful to rotate through some of the tasks so everyone gets practice and a chance to do, not only what they want to do, but what needs to be done.

7. Clarify expectations:

What rules will help us all have a good time? This prepares the way for everyone to begin thinking about expectations by beginning with specifics for one small activity. It provides the structure and support that helps most of our kids thrive. Who doesn't want to know what to expect in the future? What does everyone need to do in order to make this fun for everyone!

Step Three: Just Do It!

This is the best part! Sometimes, my expectations can be so high that I'm disappointed when things don't go as planned. The other night, during our family time, we were playing a game where each person put a funny device in their mouth and had to say phrases in a way your team could interpret. Because my current configuration of kids at home is a five-year-old girl, twin twelve-year-old boys, and a thirteen-year-old boy, finding activities everyone can do and will enjoy is not always easy.

I enticed them to the table by letting them know that I was baking brownies and that we were going to play a game while the brownies were baking. This created a doable timeline that didn't overwhelm our kids, most of whom had only joined our family a few months earlier and were still getting used to the concept of family time. I'm not going to lie: that night my husband would have much rather been in his recliner. So the first step was motivating him. Then getting the game going was like herding cats. One would get to the table and another would leave. Dividing into teams was tumultuous because everyone wanted to be on dad's team, and no one wanted to have the five-year-old play with them.

Once we got started, we had fun for a few minutes until some of the kids were laughing so hard they couldn't speak and their team members were frustrated because they couldn't earn points. If I were looking for an ideal family time, I would have thrown in the towel with disappointment. But fortunately, I have learned that moments don't have to be perfect to be memorable. We just marched forward, taking turns, laughing, making the mood lighter, or getting us back on track when needed.

Before we knew it, the timer buzzed, and everyone wanted to keep playing. After consuming brownies, everyone left the table, and as they did I heard, "That was actually fun" from pretty much everyone's mouth, including my husband. Despite the highs and lows, that was a successful family time. It's not always easy, it's usually not tranquil, it almost always takes energy you don't have, but it's always worth it. Just do it!

Putting Reset Families into Practice in Five Minutes or Less

1. If intentional family time is not part of your family routine, set a time and use the Family Connection Planning Guide to plan a meeting just to have fun as a family.
2. Select a check-in activity, decide on the ground rules for your time together, share the tasks and plan the activity.
3. Set the date, follow the directions provided above, and just do it!
4. At the end of your family time, take out the planning guide, and quickly fill out the agenda for your next time together. Each time you schedule the next meeting you are underscoring your priority to spend time together. It also helps everyone work on organizational skills and teamwork!

Further Resources, Page 178

CHAPTER 4

Setting Clear Expectations

Perhaps some of you have been reading the first three chapters of this book with a sense of urgency. *Okay, okay*, you might be thinking, *when will we get some help with changing our kids' behaviors that are driving us crazy?* Or maybe you're starting to get frustrated, thinking, *This is another one of those books that makes it seem like if we just have enough fun together, or if we're just nice enough, our kids will never misbehave!*

We promise you, this is *not* that book. We will suggest skills to help your kids manage their behavior and respond to their poor behavior choices. We understand the urgency, that sense of "things have to change now" since we are also in the midst of parenting our kids and grandkids. The challenge is to pause long enough to reflect and identify areas we can change to create a family culture that promotes close and satisfying relationships with our kids. That kind of family culture is more fun. It is the basis and prerequisite for effective discipline. Because our family culture is the foundation on which everything else is built, if that is unstable or crumbling, no system you attempt to put in place will work for very long.

We have talked about ways to make our hopes and dreams more concrete and visible. Perhaps, at this point, some of you have talked with your kids about a different vision for your family. We have also emphasized the importance of including our kids in discussions about their futures and helping them realize effective ways to use their voices. We have introduced some tools to help you engage in

SETTING CLEAR EXPECTATIONS

intentional family conversations that are inclusive and effective. It is in these conversations that our kids are able to understand how valuable they are to the family system.

If we are able to create this type of environment where our kids recognize their importance to the family and feel like they have a voice that can influence the family unit, they are more likely to engage collaboratively. In that environment of teamwork, they are able to gain the skills necessary to manage their own behavior effectively.

If you want to grow fantastic tomatoes, it doesn't start with the seeds you select. It isn't just about how you prepare the soil. It starts with where you choose to plant. How much sun will the tomatoes get? Does the soil have the nutrients tomatoes need? The answers to those questions are determined early in the process. You can have the best tomato seedling on the market, but if you plant it where there is not enough sun, your plant won't thrive.

The same is also true for any behavior-management system. You can have the best system around, but if you introduce it into a family, without carefully laying the groundwork, the outcomes are likely to be marginal at best. Relationships are the foundation of effective discipline. And building strong family relationships takes ongoing intentionality. Change is a process, and if you are applying the principles as you go, you will begin to see change, as your goals become a reality in your family.

If we have carefully tended to the soil or culture of our family, we are ready to implement practices that will help kids be effective self-managers. As we transition from creating the family culture to specific tools for behavior management, we offer a word of caution: there is no magic formula or program that comes with an unconditional guarantee. Instead, we offer a parenting approach that has been effective even when tested in some very challenging settings with kids who have experienced serious trauma.

We are confident that your family can benefit from utilizing these tools. However, the process will take time and consistency. We will continue to offer suggestions for reflection, specific activities, and conversations that you can use immediately to implement Reset Families in your home.

After taking the initial steps to create a family culture that builds strong relationships, you are ready to work on creating clear expectations. In other words, choosing the behaviors that will help you realize your family vision.

> **Stop and Reflect**
>
> As you begin to clarify your family expectations, take time to complete this personal evaluation. This will help you assess the work you have been doing to develop your family culture.
>
> 1. How *healthy* are your current *interactions* with your kids?
>   - How often do you enter into power struggles, raise your voice, or shut down and refuse to engage? How often do things get swept under the rug and ignored? What percentage of conflict is resolved in a way that adds to, rather than damages, your relationships?
>   - Have you seen change in this area as you have begun to apply some of the principles you are learning?
> 2. Have you considered one thing you would like to change about the way you interact with your kids? What do your kids say needs to change?
>   - What is one behavior you have decided to change in your response to your kids?
>   - Remember to focus on **your** behavior, not your child's behavior.
> 3. Have you attempted to make repairs?
>   - In the last chapter we talked about "necessary conversations." You may need to start your conversation about expectations with a genuine apology for the way things have been addressed in the family in the past and by expressing a desire to see a positive change in the family.

SETTING CLEAR EXPECTATIONS

> - If you have already done that, celebrate the change you are beginning to see.
> 4. On a scale of 1 to 10, how clear are your expectations for your kids right now?
> 5. On a scale of 1 to 10, how close are your kids coming to meeting your expectations?

When it comes to making our expectations clear, where do we start? There is the list of things we want them to do, like clean up after themselves and brush their teeth. And then there are the things we don't want them to do, like jumping on the furniture or hitting their brother. So as you begin to think about your expectations, remember expectations answer the question "What behaviors help us reach our hopes and dreams?"

Following, we will guide you through four activities you can use to clarify expectations with your family.

1. Brainstorming Your Family Rules
2. Using Criteria to Move from Rules to Expectations
3. Application of Expectations
4. Using the Traffic Light to Categorize Behavior Choices

Activity #1

Brainstorming Family Rules

Instructions

The first step toward clarifying your expectations is to have an intentional conversation where you brainstorm your family rules. To start, gather your kids for a brainstorming session. Keep these family conversations fun. Be willing to add an element of silly to the conversation, but be sure to capture their answers on a piece of paper or poster board for use later. Ask one of the older kids to do the writing. Ask your kids to think of as many of your family rules as possible. This is something your kids will have fun with, especially your rule-followers. If they are having trouble, prompt them with statements such as "But what about brushing your teeth or jumping on the couch?" As your kids share ideas, offer feedback like "good one" or "I forgot about that" or *Oh* boy! What a disaster if that wasn't a rule."

If the kids are hesitant, consider offering a small treat for each rule they can think of. Have a container with candy or a healthy snack available. Another option would be to offer screen minutes for every idea. The longer the list you create together, the better, so have fun. However, don't stretch this out too long; we want to keep it light and fun. It's kind of like making popcorn. You know the popcorn is done when the pops start getting too far apart.

When you complete the list, it will be *long*. Think about all the instructions you give in one day. Time to get up, get dressed, eat breakfast, clean up your dishes, brush your teeth, be kind to your brother, find your shoes, put your shoes away, grab your backpack, you can take five cookies, not a full pack of Oreos in your lunch, you know you have to do your homework, tell me ahead of time if you need a ride after school? And the list goes go on.

All those expectations, and you haven't even been awake for an hour! That's a lot of rules. No wonder our kids have a hard time remembering and following them. But all these rules are important. So what can we do? We need to simplify. We have to set clear expectations that are easy to remember. Here are some important criteria that will help you clarify your expectations:

SETTING CLEAR EXPECTATIONS

Criteria for Creating Effective Expectations

1. **Keep the number small.**
   You want no more than a handful. We suggest four to six that move you toward your goals. Too many expectations will be difficult to remember and less likely to become part of your family culture.

2. **Make them broad enough to cover a range of desired behaviors.**
   If we're only going to have a few expectations, they are going to need to be broad. Make the categories broad enough that several behaviors or rules fit under one heading. An example would be "Be responsible." That might mean that your kids hang up their coat when they come in from school, brush their teeth, take care of their belongings, and call if they are going to be late coming home. All those rules are really about responsibility.

3. **State them in positive terms, indicating the behavior you wish to see.**
   When we think about rules, it is easy to get a whole list of *don'ts*: no running, no screaming, no unkind words, no swearing, and no back talk. But that is going counter to what we are trying to achieve here. In many arenas, rules are stated in the negative, like the circle with a line through it over guns or drugs, for example. Rules stated from the negative feel power laden and controlling. They describe what has to stop, but don't give suggestions about how to replace that behavior.
   It works best to speak to the kids from the positive. What does positive behavior look like? You will need to give them examples of what you mean. You may incorporate the negative example as you are talking about this with your kids. An example: put your backpack on the hook inside the back door when you come home from school. Don't throw it on the kitchen floor. But your "posted expectations" are best started from the positive.

4. Make each expectation explicit, concrete, and agreed on.

When we are dealing with a specific area of challenge with our kids, it is easy to think that "Be responsible" says enough. For example, if you are working with your child on being responsible by getting homework done, you may say to yourself, *That should be enough.* For some kids, that will be enough, but for your perfectionist you may need to say something like "When you get home from school, you may take thirty minutes to relax. Then work on your homework, finishing any assignments that are due the following day. When you are finished, check it off with me and then you can have free time until dinner." By being explicit, you have helped your child understand what it looks like to be responsible. So when they do something other than the agreed-on routine, you have a shared concrete expectation to point to.

You know what your children need, so work with them to choose the best plan to achieve the goal, then state it as clearly as possible as in the example above. Notice the emphasis on working with them. They often know what they need better than you do, so take the time to work it out together. The advantage of taking the time to work through the expectation with them is you are re-teaching the expectation in a way they can be successful. If you paint a picture for your kids of the behavior you want to see, it will be easier for them to succeed.

My son should be an attorney. If there is a loophole, he'll find it. When he was an adolescent, he had a terrible habit of leaving his socks in the living room. I don't like feet, especially teenage-boy feet after sports turnout. And by extension, I don't like dirty socks! Day after day I reminded him not to leave his dirty socks in the living room. Eventually, he stopped leaving his socks in the living room, and I was thrilled. But then, I walked past his bedroom door. The socks had simply migrated to the floor of his room.

When I brought this up with him he said, "You just said not to leave my socks in the living room." Unfortunately, he had me there. My expectation was not specific and concrete enough. Rather than painting a picture of what I wanted—"Please be responsible and put your dirty clothes in the hamper"—I just told him what not to do.

And technically, he was obeying my request. He wasn't leaving his socks in the living room. When we paint a picture of what we want to see, it communicates a clear pathway to our goals and avoids loophole bargaining.

In the first activity, we encouraged you to brainstorm your family rules, and you likely ended with a long list. It is hard to imagine how we get from the long list of rules, to a list that meets the criteria we just talked about. How in the world do we take our current expectations, and boil them down to just a few that are easy to remember and empower our kids to be self-managers?

The goal is to focus on four to six expectations that are broad enough to encompass almost every desired behavior. But you want them to be simple enough to be easily remembered so that they become a part of your family culture. Also remember to state those expectations in positive terms.

The Reset Family Expectations meet the criteria we identified. We encourage you to use these as you get started clarifying your expectations. Later you may choose to add to or adjust them as your family grows and changes.

Be Respectful—Respect is about valuing another person or even yourself. Family expectations like, treat others the way you want to be treated, use kind words, use your manners and say things build up rather than tear down, can all be summed up with *Be Respectful*. Notice that it is identifying the behavior you want to see.

Be Responsible—Responsibility is about taking care of the things that are within your power, control, or ability to manage. Family rules like do your homework, do your chores, pick up after yourself, tell me what you need in advance and brush your teeth can be summed up with *Be Responsible*.

Be a Listener—Listening is not only about hearing, but also about processing information, engaging, and even obeying by following directions. Family rules like listen the first time, follow directions, wait while others speak, and obey the rules fit nicely under the category of *Be a Listener*.

Be Safe—Safety is about keeping yourself and others from harm emotionally, physically, socially, and spiritually. Safety is about more than protecting your physical body. It's also about guarding your heart and mind from things that would threaten your emotional, social, and spiritual health. Family rules around drugs, alcohol, entertainment, video games, stranger danger, conversations about sexuality or looking before you cross the street are all expectations that can be summarized with *Be Safe*.

Be Trustworthy— Trustworthiness is about being honest, reliable and dependable. Family rules like always tell the truth, respect others' personal property, ask before you take something, and do what you say you will do, can be addressed with the expectation that family members *Be Trustworthy*.

> **Stop and Reflect**
>
> If you were to select one expectation to implement, which would do the most to make your interactions at home more peaceful and family relationships stronger?

Activity #2

Using Criteria to Move from Rules to Expectations

In the second activity, you will go back to where you left off brainstorming rules with your family. You will simplify and organize this list of rules to fit under specific expectations that empower your kids to be self-managers.

SETTING CLEAR EXPECTATIONS

Instructions

Plan a family time and remember to make it fun. Take the list of "Family Rules" you created during your brainstorming activity. Use a copy of the Reset Family Expectations sheet, listing the five categories. (See example, pg. 181 in Future References.) Working with your kids create five posters or sheets of paper, each with one of the expectations written on the top "Be Respectful," "Be Responsible," "Be a Listener," "Be Safe," "Be Trustworthy." You may want to write the brief description on top as well, to keep you on track. You could also do this on one sheet of paper or a white board with the five categories across the top. Our guess is that every family rule you have can fit into one of those categories and some of them can even fit into more than one category.

Next take your "rules poster" and have the kids take turns reading the rule, with help if needed. Then work together as a family to decide which category it belongs in. If old enough, the child who read the rule can write it on the appropriate sheet. If not, you can write it under the appropriate category. For example, someone may have suggested "clothes are put in the laundry." Ask them what expectation they think this fits under? When they figure it out, encourage them by saying something like "You're right! That would fit under *Be Responsible.*" Finally, if that seems too overwhelming, make sure you leave room before each rule and when you are done with the brainstorm, ask the kids to help you label each rule with the appropriate expectation. No matter how you do it, the important thing is that you do it with the kids, so they feel they contributed.

When you finish with this activity you have begun to lay the foundation for accountability by clarifying your expectations. You can build on that foundation using this language of expectations around your home. That's how it will become a part of your family culture. Instead of just saying, "Pick up your shoes," you will say, "Be responsible and pick up your shoes." In each interaction, you are reinforcing one of the family expectations.

This common language used repeatedly is powerful. As our daughter was growing, we knew it was time to add the expectation of "be trustworthy" when she discovered the temptation to lie to get out of trouble. I could ask her if she did something multiple times, and she might deny it. But when I said, "Are you being trustworthy?" the keyword *trustworthy* caused her to pause and, most often, tell the truth at that point. It may feel like you are being very repetitive at first, but as you continue to reinforce the behaviors with that language, you may find that you need to use it less often.

Expectations that are clear and easy to articulate also create a strong sense of security. Kids feel like they know what you want from them. I remember when our twins moved it with us. They were ten at the time. About a month after they moved in I took them for a doctor visit. The doctor asked them how they were doing adjusting to the new home, as they had been having a hard time in their previous home. The boys reported that they were doing well. The doctor asked why they thought they were doing so well. One of the boys said that, as a matter of fact, it was because they knew the expectations. When the doctor asked what they were, the boys easily rattled off: be responsible, be respectful, be safe, be a listener, be trustworthy. The doctor was impressed, and so was I.

The boys felt empowered to be successful because they knew what behaviors we were looking for. When they weren't sure whether something was allowed in our house or not, they had a filter to pass it through. They didn't have to learn through experience by getting into trouble or being told not to do something, although there is always some of that. Instead, they could ask themselves, would that be responsible? Is that respectful? And they could figure out how to do what was right. That reflection is far more empowering than having the parent constantly reminding them or, worse yet, nagging them. The more you incorporate these expectations into your day-to-day conversations, the more quickly they will become a part of your shared language, shared understanding, a part of your family culture.

You have done the hard work to brainstorm all your family rules. Then you worked to categorize each of the rules under one of the five Reset Family Expectations. You will need to take one more step to make this applicable for your family.

SETTING CLEAR EXPECTATIONS

Activity #3

Application of Expectations

Instructions

Plan one more family meeting time and have an intentional conversation about choosing the expectation you want to focus on first. Use the "Setting Behavior Expectations" sheet (page 181 in "Further References") to figure out where to start. The questions on the sheet might be all you need to get started. What behavior in our family would you like to change? This may be something all of you have to work on together. Maybe there is too much yelling and angry voices. You may be part of that, and it is beneficial for you to take the lead admitting your part in it.

After you ask the question "What behavior would you like to change?" the next question and your response to it is crucial. That question is, "What would happen instead?" The kids will have some great ideas to offer here, and you can chime in with yours. Make sure you are able to express what you want in explicit, concrete terms that you can all agree on. It may look something like, we agree that instead of yelling or using an angry voice, we will "take a break," ask ourselves why we feel that way, and think about what we want to say in an appropriate way. We want our kids to use their voices after they have taken time to identify and evaluate their feelings, so their response can be heard.

This type of clarification of your expectations will be a skill you will come back to over and over again. As you discover that your kids don't have clarity on an expectation, you will want to teach them the expectations using clear, explicit, concrete language. At times you can ask the kids to take the lead in asking the questions and clarifying. Then, your children will understand the expectation and you will find it much easier to hold them accountable.

Recently, it became clear that our kids didn't thoroughly understand our expectation of respecting each other. In order to help them better understand, we stated our expectation in clear, concrete terms, and then began to hold them accountable to that expectation. We began with the statement, "In our home, we will be respectful to one another. This means we do not insult, put-down, name call, or gang up on each other." You might think this is a given, but with three seventh-grade boys in the house, we needed to focus on this area for a while to break some bad habits that were beginning to form.

> **Stop and Reflect**
>
> Setting clear, agreed-upon expectation is the key to helping our kids become self-managers. Once these expectations are clear, the steps of the behavior-management system will make more sense. So be sure to take time now to complete each of the expectations activities.
>
> Which expectation has your family decided to work on first?

Hopefully you have identified one expectation that you are ready to focus on in the coming days and weeks. As you apply the principle of making expectations clear, you will need a way to help your kids know how they are doing at meeting the expectations you have decided on together. That's where the traffic light comes in.

Do you have a back seat driver? My youngest is still in a car seat. If the light turns green and we aren't moving, she is telling me it's time to move regardless of the cars in front of us that our still stopped, or our need to yield to oncoming traffic! From a very young age, kids can understand the traffic light. How many of us played "red light, green light" growing up? In Reset Families, we use this familiar symbol to begin to provide feedback to our kids about how well they are doing meeting the family expectations.

The traffic-light tool will help you integrate and reinforce the expectations you have been working on together by providing common language and giving you a tool for consistent feedback. I mentioned earlier I have a back seat driver on my hands. The other day, we were running late for a meeting. I was at the back of a long line of

SETTING CLEAR EXPECTATIONS

traffic. I was coming to the front of the line just as the light turned yellow. I know the right thing to do would have been to slow to a stop, but I really didn't want to wait through another set of lights with three lanes of traffic in every direction. So instead, I accelerated and made it through just as the light turned red. As I was doing so, I hear from the backseat, "Mom, yellow means slow down, not speed up." Good thing I still have more than a decade until she can learn to drive. Clearly, I wasn't setting the best example, but it does make a great illustration.

The traffic light is a well-known and understood symbol. The imagery is clear. Green means "go," yellow means use "caution," and red means "stop." In Reset Families, we use this common language to help our kids identify what kind of behavior choice they are making and understand *what* the consequences of their behavior choice might be. Along with a common language, the traffic-light tool helps you give your child consistent feedback about how they are doing to meet the expectations you have agreed on as a family. It also helps you label the child's behavior choice rather than labeling them as a person. It emphasizes the behavior that needs to change rather than labeling the child in a negative or deficient way.

So how exactly does the system work? We have reimagined the traffic light for use with Reset Families. You will notice that the arrangement of the light appears to be upside down. That is intentional to help emphasize the importance of focusing on the positive. In addition, there is an additional green light. The lights represent four categories of behavior:

The Traffic Light

Super Green- Above and beyond!

Green- Meeting expectations

Yellow- Not meeting expectations

Red- unsafe behavior

Super Green: Going Above and Beyond

This could be defined as extraordinary behavior. It requires great effort. It is selfless. Super green behavior is going out of your way for another person, conquering a personal fear, choosing not to react to a serious offense like when brother hits you and you don't hit back, but rather, asking for help from an adult. What's super green for one kid, because it requires extraordinary effort for them, may not be super green for another because it comes more naturally.

When your child demonstrates super green behavior, it's important to notice and verbally reward that behavior. Praise is best when it is specific and tied to the behavior you want to see. You may say something like, "Wow! That must have been really difficult for you to come home after a busy day at school and choose to jump into your homework rather than playing your video game. Thanks for being responsible. That was definitely super green." Another example: "Thanks for being trustworthy by sticking up for your brother when he was being bullied. I can tell you are working hard to help us make change with that super green choice."

Notice how those statements validate the hard work the child is doing as well as tying them to the expectation with the traffic-light color. Doing that helps you reinforce both the expectation and specifically describes the behavior you want to see. It works best to give the reinforcement immediately after the behavior. It just needs a simple, momentary celebration. Avoid the temptation to give extravagant praise that will likely seem insincere to the child. If there are times you neglect to reinforce the behavior, don't worry. Pick it up the next time. An intermittent schedule of reinforcement tends to work best. Just remember to keep balance by noticing the positive with holding them accountable for behavior that doesn't meet expectations.

Green: Meeting Expectations

Green behavior is when your child is being responsible, respectful, a listener, safe, or trustworthy. They are doing what we expect them to do. It can be easy to take green behavior for granted. After all, it's simply doing what they are supposed to do. When your child is demonstrating green behavior, it's great to offer specific verbal praise. Just as with super green behavior, the praise will help to reinforce that positive behavior that you want to continue to see. You might say, "Gabriel, thanks for being responsible and doing your chores" or "Samantha, great job being respectful and using your manners."

Stop and Reflect:

Think about a few super green and green behavior choices that you could reinforce this week

As you get started teaching your kids this system, you will want to focus on what is right, rather than always pointing out what's wrong. A great way to do this is by noticing the positive behaviors that you see. By spending time to let them know you notice their efforts to try and demonstrate the characteristics you value as a family, you are communicating to your children that you value them and the effort they are making.

This form of feedback may feel redundant at times, and you may wonder about the effectiveness of your words of praise. However, continuing to recognize those behaviors, even when you don't see immediate results will increase the likelihood of those behaviors becoming your child's default behavior, rather than just a hopeful dream for your kids.

And that's all there is to it. If you just praise the behaviors you want to see in your kids, they'll stop making negative behavior choices, grow up to be great self-managers, realize their full potential, and you'll live happily ever after. Unfortunately, that's not quite true. At least it hasn't been true in our years of combined parenting experience. It would be ideal if kids were compliant and able to manage their behavior all the time as we simply reinforce them for exhibiting green and super green choices, but that is not realistic. That is where the yellow and red lights help us.

When the moment comes that your kids are not meeting expectations, you need a way to remind them of expectations you've agreed to and then have a consistent response to the behavior that is not meeting expectations. We will delve into that later in the next chapter, but first let's finish exploring the traffic-light tool, specifically the behavioral choices represented by the yellow and red lights.

Yellow: Not Meeting Expectations

Yellow behavior choices violate the family expectations, take the child off course from accomplishing family hopes and dreams, but are not unsafe behaviors. Most undesirable behavior falls in this category. You *always* respond to yellow behavior choices with Redirection, the approach we will explore later.

SETTING CLEAR EXPECTATIONS

Red: Red behavior Is Unsafe Behavior

Safety involves not only physical safety but also social, emotional, and spiritual safety. A red behavior may be unsafe only to the person engaging in the behavior, or it may be a safety risk to others. Whether it harms others or not, unsafe behavior falls in this red category. You always respond to unsafe behavior by intervening immediately. That may mean that you step between two kids where one is hitting or otherwise being violent to another saying something like, "It is unsafe behavior to hit your brother." Or you may need to hold a child who was running toward the road, saying, "It is unsafe for me to let you run when you run toward the road." After you have deescalated the situation, you will address the behavior utilizing the third step of the redirection process, which we will cover in detail later in the next chapter.

We will get to the how-to part of integrating the traffic-light system with the redirection system. First, let's practice categorizing children's behavior into each of the color categories, much the same way as we did with family rules.

Activity #4

Using the Traffic Light to Categorize Behavior Choices

Instructions:

Plan one more family meeting time where you introduce the traffic-light system. This will be easy for most kids to understand and relate to, so it won't require a great deal of time. Using the Behavior Choices Sheet (see page 182 in "Further References"), mark each behavior with the appropriate color designation (SG – super green; G – green; Y – yellow, and R – red). Work together with your kids on this activity as you teach them the traffic-light system.

You may find that it is not always easy to categorize the behaviors, and that family members don't always agree which is "yellow" or "red," or "green" and "super green" for that matter. The designations may vary by family as well. In some families the use of slang or worse may be yellow, and for others that may be an automatic red behavior. This exercise will help you discuss this as a family and clearly establish the expectations for your family.

Not only does this traffic-light system give your kids feedback about how they measure up with the expectations you have set as a family, it is a great reminder for both parents and kids. It reminds us as parents that we must have specific responses to each of the four types of behavior choices if we expect to be effective with our discipline. It is also a crucial part of the consistent feedback component of Reset Families.

> **Stop and Reflect**
>
> We have covered a lot of information so far, and this would be a great time to pause your reading and ask yourself a few questions. Have you laid the foundation necessary for effective discipline? Remember, relationship is the key. Have you reflected on your default parenting style and become more aware of your triggers? Has your family begun to dream together? Taking the time to create a shared family vision for the kind of family you'd like to be? If you did that, don't forget to come back to it over and over again. Maybe every Sunday at dinner until you get tired of it, then maybe once or twice a month. Don't let your family vision become just an activity you did once. In order for it to be a part of your family culture, you'll need to revisit it often.
>
> How are family times going? Are you finding times to intentionally have fun together as a family? It does not have to be a long time, but it does have to be intentional. Our good intentions rarely accomplish all we hope. Instead, we must intentionally make space for the things we value most. It is out of a culture of connection that we begin to work toward our goals and vision together. Setting clear expectations is a necessary step toward empowering our kids and being the family we want to be.

SETTING CLEAR EXPECTATIONS

In the next chapter, we are going to jump into a system that you can use to respond to your kids' behavior choices. The next couple of chapters will help you as parents respond, rather than react to behavior that fails to meet the family expectations. They will also empower your kids to be self-managers. The chapters will give you the tools to end power struggles, see positive behavior change, and live with less chaos.

The system is not perfect, it doesn't always work every time, but we believe it's a great tool for the job. *But* don't turn the page until you're ready. Anything we try that is new to us works best when it is built on a strong foundation, a foundation you will build as you implement a pattern of self-reflection time. It requires a commitment to a shared family vision, establishing a rhythm of intentional connections, and committing to clarifying expectations.

Just a word of encouragement: read the book as fast as you'd like, but when it comes to implementation, implement all the pieces. Ideally, one week at a time. But even if you do it all at once, do it *all* at once. Don't leave out the relational foundation. It is the harmony of relationships and accountability for behavior choices that produces the greatest results. Creating a strong connection with our kids is the beginning of effective discipline.

RESET FAMILIES

Putting Reset Families into Practice in Five Minutes or Less:

Hopefully by now, noticing the positive behaviors has become a habit for you and part of your family culture. Continue giving specific, concrete words of praise immediately after the behaviors that you want to see. This will help both you and your child see how they are making progress toward the family vision.

Check to see how often you are noticing your child's behavior triggers and suggesting that they "take a break." Encourage them to request it as well.

We've introduced four activities you can do with your family in this chapter. With older kids you may be able to get through more than one at a time, but these are more than five-minute exercises. It is more important that you complete activities and then implement them fully, than to race through and lose your way.

1. Family Activity Number 1 and Number 2 can generally be completed in a single family meeting time and make better sense when done together. Try to get through the brainstorming of your family rules and then categorize each one under one of the five Reset Family Expectations.
2. Family Activity Number 3 – Work together with your kids to choose the expectation you want to focus on first as a family. Using the "Setting Behavior Expectations" sheet (pg. 181 in "Further References") clarify the expectation.
- Describe the behavior you want to see in concrete and specific language.
- Make sure everyone understands and agrees. You may want to consider a written contract.
3. Family Activity Number 4 – Teach your kids the traffic-light system and begin using the language with them as focus for now on green and super green behavior choices. Complete the Behavior Choices Sheet.

Further Resources, Page 180

Chapter 5

Integrating Expectations with Behavior Redirection

In the last chapter we took a hard look at expectations and the challenge of making them clear in our family. We also introduced the traffic-light tool. This allows you to let your kids know how they are doing at meeting the family expectations. To this point you have focused on noticing the super green" and green behaviors and have been responding to those behaviors at times with specific, concrete, and authentic praise. But what do you do with the behaviors that fail to meet your family expectations? In this chapter we will look at responding to yellow and red behavior choices.

Responding to Behaviors that Do Not Meet Expectations: Preparing Our Kids for Redirection

When our kids fail to meet expectations, we need a tool to respond to their choice. A great way to respond to behavior that is off target is by using the "Take a Break" suggestion we made in Chapter One. By being in tune to your kids' big emotions and reminding them to "Take a Break," you actually set them up to meet the expectations you chosen to work on and to give them the first opportunity to be self-managers.

When we wrote about "Take a Break," we began encouraging you to notice your child's big emotions and help them express them appropriately. At various times during the day, our kids are at the point that they are at risk of poor behavior choices (yellow behavior) but have not stepped over that line yet. You know what those moments look like. The tension begins to build as your child gets stuck on a homework problem or stuck on the idea of hating homework. Or you can tell when the older sibling has just about had their fill of the younger sibling pestering them.

Sometimes, it has nothing to do with what's going on at home at the moment but rather something that happened at school or something the child is dreading. And it's not always negative emotions that boil over. Sometimes excitement or anticipation can bubble a bit too far. If we tune in, we can often recognize when big emotions are about to boil over into yellow, or even red behaviors and help to avoid that boil over.

What we are trying to avoid is what is often referred to as *emotional flooding*. As the term suggests, your child is overcome by a flood of emotions in reaction to fear or overwhelming stress. Often, the reaction is based on information that is faulty, like a perceived danger or slight by a sibling. The reaction occurs and overrides the part of the brain that would allow the child to check and see if the feelings are accurate, or if the situation warrants that intense response.

Once your child is emotionally flooded, they really can't be rational. They need time to come down from the intensity of the reaction and gain control of those big emotions. That is where "Take a Break" comes in to help them pause, identify the big emotion, and think about an appropriate response before they become emotionally flooded and make a poor choice.

Remember, this is not to be confused with "time out," it's a privilege, not a punishment. Taking a break can even be fun and definitely relaxing.

Now let's expand on "Take a Break" a bit. We will show you how to use it as part of our three-step system where we redirect our child's behavior and help them become self-managers.

"Take a Break" is the first step toward your child becoming a self-manager. *It* will help kids redirect their own behavior as we teach them to pause long enough to think about an appropriate response to big emotions. Practicing this skill will help you and your child recognize when trouble is brewing. It allows you to help your child identify signs that they are heading off track and encourage them to take a break before they make a poor choice.

There are several things you can do to help your child recognize what is happening in their body as they become overwhelmed or agitated. As you practice taking a break, you and your child can learn to identify what happens physically in their body in such situations. You may ask them questions like "What do you feel in your body? What signs do you see [sigh, clinched fist, restlessness, blurting]?" Learning to do this early will help your child not only in difficult family situations, but also at school and in life in general. This is a lifelong skill, and once the child has learned to identify those big emotions, they can learn to manage them successfully.

Finally, using "Take a Break" helps your child avoid escalation. The problem has stayed small, and they are in charge of managing their emotions and behavior rather than you having to enter into the three-step redirection process to manage their behavior for them.

Just to review a bit, as a parent, you know your child well. You can often sense when they are becoming overwhelmed or frustrated. They haven't failed to meet expectations yet, but you know it's only a matter of time. That's the time to use "Take a Break."

How Does Take a Break Work?

We spent a great deal of time on "Take a Break" in the first chapter and how to teach your child the skill. Now let's take a look at exactly how it works to introduce the redirection system. As you begin to implement "Take a Break" with redirection, take time to remind them they can request it, or that you might suggest it. Also, they should express their feelings appropriately and ask permission for a break. You can grant permission verbally or give them a pass. Encourage them to use it so they can manage themselves long before they lose control.

Make certain that you keep the break structured. If you have not already designated a "Take a Break" location, it will be important to do that so that as we integrate it with redirection. This is not a place where there are toys to distract them, but possibly a squishy ball, fidget widget, or some other handheld manipulative to help them relax and focus their energy. Sometimes a break location may include a beanbag chair, hammock swing, or even a pod or small pop-up tent. One of the ways that "Take a Break" feels more like an opportunity than a punishment is to have some options on hand to help your child take a breath and get ready to go back to whatever they're facing.

Stop and Reflect:

What options might work in your family? Some of the best "take a break" options we've used are:

- Pinwheels: breathe in through your nose and out through your mouth as you blow the wheel.
- A favorite song (and a way to play it) they can just listen or even dance along. When the song is over, they return to what they were doing before.
- A Simple coloring sheet and crayons.
- A book of riddles.
- A challenge list:
  - Place both hands against the wall and push (don't pound) with all your might.
  - Sit in your chair with your feet off the floor, and using only your hands, try to lift the chair you are sitting in.
  - Interlace your fingers (like you're praying) and push both hands together in front of your chest. Can you push with all your might for thirty seconds?
  - Do ten push-ups.
  - Try twenty sit-ups.
  - Bust out thirty jumping jacks.

EXPECTATIONS AND REDIRECTION

> - A hug . . . sometimes I stop what I'm doing too and ask them if they just need a hug, want a snuggle, or if they (for older kids) could use a bear hug . . . Then I give them a squeeze and remind them they've got this. (Be careful not to fall into coaching or problem-solving here, that would undermine the break.)

Part of the structure you provide for "Take a Break" is time limits. The break should last no longer than two to five minutes. Then the child must come back and engage using an appropriate response to the situation. Do not allow this to become a "divert and forget" strategy. You may want to give them a timer that will remind them when the break is over. By allowing them to be in charge of the timer, you are adding one more layer of support for them to manage their own behavior. Two to five minutes will not be enough if your child is overwhelmed and has already flooded before the break was suggested. This is why it's important to learn to recognize feelings early. Remember, once someone has "flipped their lid," it takes about twenty minutes of distraction for the physiology to return to normal. They need time for their pulse to slow, their muscles to relax, and chemicals that have swarmed their brain to retreat. Take a break is effective before emotional flooding occurs. If we don't catch the feelings in time, we may have to wait longer.

Even with all your best efforts to help them take the time to stop, reflect, and make a positive behavior choice, there will be times they refuse to use "Take a Break" and manage their behavior. That is their choice. If they proceed to make a yellow behavior choice (not meeting expectations), then we implement the three-step redirection process.

Redirection is the skill we use to redirect our kids' behavior and give them not only the opportunity, but also cues so that they can learn to manage their own behavior. If you are using the traffic-light symbol, the redirection process is used only in response to yellow behavior choices, or those that fail to meet the family expectations. Behavior that is disrespectful, irresponsible, and not trustworthy or fails to follow direction is yellow behavior. By using redirection, we are attempting to stop the undesired behaviors by reminding the child that they can manage their own behavior rather than having us step in to manage it for them. Redirection empowers your kids, teaches them the skills to manage their own behavior, and reinforces those skills when they have trouble remembering how to do it.

How Does Redirection Work?

Let's quickly review what we have talked about so far. We introduced the traffic-light symbol and the meaning attached to each color. We emphasized the importance of reinforcing the behavior we want to see by giving specific verbal praise for green and super green behaviors. We talked about the importance of "Take a Break." This is a tool that may help your child pause, reflect, and turn their behavior around, thereby avoiding the need for the three-step redirection process. We want to help our kids notice the big emotions and try to manage them *before* bad behavior choices erupt. However, if they are unable to manage their behavior, we need to use redirection. That helps them gain the skills they need so we no longer have to step in every time.

In redirection, you become a partner, helping your child become an effective self-manager. Ideally, our kids make green and super green behavior choices all the time, but nobody's perfect, so when they struggle we come alongside them with reminders that help them get themselves back on track.

Rather than threaten or nag them into positive behavior choices, we nudge them in the right direction, confident that they can recognize the yellow behavior and turn things around. They are strong, smart and capable, plus we're not always going to be there to help them make the right choice. Instead, we want to help them become self-managers. We do that by consistently responding to unmet expectations or yellow behavior, with redirection.

EXPECTATIONS AND REDIRECTION

To see the redirection process in action, visit www.resetfamilies.org and search for Redirection Video.

> **Three Reminders to Self-Manage**
>
> You have already tried to help them identify and manage their big emotions with "take a break"
>
> When they are still unsuccessful...
>
> Proceed to Three Reminders
>
> Step One - Non-Verbal Que
> Step Two - Precision Request
> Step Three - Reset
>
> ☐ Give the same cue EVERY time and only ONCE
> ☐ Walk away - Don't engage
> ☐ Give the child adequate time to manage their behavior

Step One – Nonverbal Cue

As soon as you notice that your child is not meeting a behavior expectation, it is time to give them a nonverbal cue. It is easy to fall into the habit of waiting to see what will happen, but that most often results in the situation escalating and becoming a bigger challenge. An early and consistent response helps ensure that your child will learn to manage their behavior before it gets out of hand. You will need to train your child to the redirection process and decide together on the cue you wish to use for each step.

One nonverbal cue we have used is *three knocks*. It works well because you can use it anywhere, and the child doesn't have to be looking at you to pick up on the cue. However, the knocking escalates some children, so you may want to use your "look." Every parent has one that lets the children know it is time for them to change their behavior. Think about your look and make certain that it is one of expectation, with raised eyebrows, rather than a frown that may indicate harshness. Some families choose to use a hand signal, and that works too. Just make sure the signal is encouraging of positive behavior and not harsh or critical. A finger wag might feel condemning rather than hopeful. Instead, taping your temple with a smile encouraging them to stop and think might be a signal that conveys positive expectation. Whatever cue you decide to use, decide it together. That creates buy in and makes sure your children know that you will use that every time you are reminding them to stop, think, and manage their own behavior.

As you teach your child about the redirection cues, say something like "When I knock, or you see me give you the 'look' you should be thinking, *What do I need to do right now to manage my behavior?*" The reason we start with a nonverbal cue is to make every effort not to shame or embarrass the child. If that happens, it is easy for them to escalate or become defiant. Our goal is to gently remind them to manage their behavior in a way we would prefer to be reminded. The nonverbal cue works well even when their friends are over.

After you give the nonverbal cue, walk away. Do not engage in any discussion. Go right back to what you were doing, or get engaged with one of your children who is making the right behavior choice. Give the other child specific positive feedback about what they are doing that is meeting expectations. By doing that, you are giving the child who is struggling with making a good choice a clue about what you want them to do. Another example: You may have just asked your child to pick up the crayons and get ready to leave for ballet practice. When they have trouble complying, you would give them the nonverbal cue and then walk away going over to her sister and saying, "Thanks for being responsible by putting the crayons away so that we are not late for ballet."

It's very important that you do not get drawn into discussion with the child you have given the cue. At first, this is very difficult to do. Most of us have become accustomed to hovering to make sure we are understood or to help ensure we are preserving the relationship. Don't fall into that trap. It is almost certain to result in a power

EXPECTATIONS AND REDIRECTION

struggle and opens the door to negative dialog. Make sure your body language and facial expressions are calm and relaxed. That demeanor will reassure them that they are not in trouble. Just like we don't want to nag with our words, we also don't want to nag with our cues or body language. Give the nonverbal cue once, walk away, and give the child space to respond.

Give your child adequate time to make a good choice and manage their own behavior. This will vary with the age of your child, from thirty seconds for a preschool child to one or two minutes for a school-age child. Generally speaking, the younger the child, the shorter the time allowed between the cues, so that they do not get distracted but can connect the cue with the behavior you are requesting. Watch carefully for signs of compliance, and allow time for them to turn to a more positive behavior choice.

If the child doesn't respond by changing the behavior or begins to escalate, go to the next step. Remember to stay calm and use a tone of voice that speaks to the child of your confidence in their ability to make a good behavior choice.

Step Two: Precision Request

The precision request is a verbal cue that isn't dependent on behavior. You don't say, "Stop jumping on the couch" or "don't run in the house." Why? Because your child already knows they shouldn't be jumping on the couch. You've told them lots of times. Instead pick one simple, short phrase and use it every time. We use "Make it green," referring back to the traffic light symbol where green is meeting expectations.

Your family can choose the cue that's a good fit for you. Remember, letting your kids have input helps create buy in. Besides, it can be a lot of fun. Some kids like to use a nonsense word. Whatever you choose as a family, the cue should be short, used the same way every time and only used once.

Let's say it's time for dinner. You've asked your son to set the table, but he is playing his video game. You are sure that he heard you, but he is now ignoring your request. The temptation is to ask him again, this time with more emphasis. Instead, you walk over, give the nonverbal cue (e.g., three knocks), and walk away. He begins to protest, but rather than responding, you simply go back to finishing dinner and give him time to make the right choice.

After about a minute, you notice he is still playing the video game and making no progress toward setting the table. Move into proximity, say his name, give the precision request (e.g., "Make it green"), and walk away. As tempting as it is to stand there and nag with your body language until he complies, walk away and go back to what you were doing. Although you may want to repeat yourself, "I said, *make it green*" for emphasis, we give each cue only once. The space between the cues is space for your child to be a self-manager. The space in between is also the space where we are most often drawn into power struggles. But in the same way you don't have a tug-of-war if the other team won't pick up the rope, you also won't have a power struggle if you refuse to be drawn into the discussion.

The process is exactly the same with each request. Once the cue is given, walk away and move on. *Do not* get drawn into a discussion. Give your child adequate time to make a good choice and manage their behavior. On occasion, your child may not respond to the first two reminders. In that case, it's time for Step Three—Reset.

Step Three – Reset

If you have given the nonverbal cue and the precision request, allowing adequate time and the child is still not meeting expectations, instruct the child to "head to reset." Just like the reset button on your cell phone or video game system, reset is an opportunity to clear the junk and start fresh. It is important to emphasize that they are not in trouble but need time to reflect on the choice they made and come up with a plan to make a better choice.

Just as with the first two cues, give the instruction with anticipation and hopefulness. No need to go overboard in your tone of voice. Often, we are tempted to be harsh in our instruction to head to reset, while telling our kids they aren't in trouble. If it sounds like trouble, you're going to have a hard time convincing them otherwise.

EXPECTATIONS AND REDIRECTION

Remember, reset is the third reminder. It's the third opportunity. You are still partnering with your child to help them manage their own behavior. Reset is a space you create for them to get rid of distractions and focus on what they need to do differently to manage their behavior at that moment. Give the direction to "head to reset" only once. Immediately walk away and even though it is tempting, don't get drawn into a discussion. In the next chapter we will give you some suggestions on setting up your actual reset location.

There will be a time for discussion, but that will happen once they are at the reset location and are calm. Be sure to give them adequate time to make it their idea to head to reset, rather than using power at this point. We want to provide enough time with cues and positive support to make a good choice on their own. In the next chapter we will describe what happen at reset, but for now let's focus on the three steps.

It's important that you don't wait until you are exasperated, frustrated, or annoyed to start the redirection process. The goal is for this system of redirection to become your response to all yellow behavior, all the time. Now, we realize that's going to take a lot of practice but the result of using this system over time is a child who is able to identify their big emotions and manage their own behavior more often.

The Redirection Pattern

Let's talk about the similarities of each of the three steps:

- Give the same cue every time and give the cue only once.
- Walk away. Don't engage in any dialogue.
- Give your child adequate time to manage their behavior.

Do you notice the pattern? Give the cue the same way every time. Give it only once and don't nag. Walk away and don't engage, while making sure they have adequate time to make a positive behavior choice. If you have trained them adequately, they know what they need to do once the cue is given. The simple structure of the three cues applied with consistency will lead to change. Let's take a look at each of the similarities separately.

1. **Use the same cue every time and give it only once.**

    We use a nonverbal cue, precision request, and reset cues containing as few words as possible, because the more we talk, the less value our words have. If you keep from engaging verbally, you won't end up in an argument with a child who likes to "split hairs." You say, "Stop jumping on the couch" and they say, "I'm not jumping, I'm bouncing." Using the same cue every time like a broken record provides consistency and structure that signals you are committed to the system. More importantly, that you are committed to providing the support they need in a way they can count on. And finally, that you believe they are capable of knowing right from wrong and making positive behavior choices.

    Like we said before, you don't want to nag silently any more than you should nag verbally, so don't be tempted to give the cue more than once. It is easy to second guess the system and say to ourselves, "He must not have heard me" and then we give the cue a second time. This undermines the system and suggests to your child that you may not be serious about the way the system is used. Giving the cue only once reassures them that you mean what you say and that you are confident that they can manage their own behavior.

2. **Walk away and don't engage.**

    It is critical that you walk away or go right back to what you were doing, so that you are not drawn into a power struggle with the child who is looking to argue. Remember, once they have complied and head for reset, they will have the opportunity to tell their side of the story. It is important to emphasize this when you are training your child to the system.

    Training and consistency are critical here, as well as reminding your child that you care about what they have to say. They need to know that you will always create a space for them to share their thoughts and feelings. However, you want the behavior that is not meeting expectations to stop first. Then they will have the chance to talk about it.

wrong. A great way to do this is by noticing the positive behaviors that you see. By spending time to let them know you notice their efforts to try and demonstrate the characteristics you value as a family, you are communicating to your children that you value them and the effort they are making.

This form of feedback may feel redundant at times, and you may wonder about the effectiveness of your words of praise. However, continuing to recognize those behaviors, even when you don't see immediate results will increase the likelihood of those behaviors becoming your child's default behavior, rather than just a hopeful dream for your kids.

And that's all there is to it. If you just praise the behaviors you want to see in your kids, they'll stop making negative behavior choices, grow up to be great self-managers, realize their full potential, and you'll live happily ever after. Unfortunately, that's not quite true. At least it hasn't been true in our years of combined parenting experience. It would be ideal if kids were compliant and able to manage their behavior all the time as we simply reinforce them for exhibiting green and super green choices, but that is not realistic. That is where the yellow and red lights help us.

When the moment comes that your kids are not meeting expectations, you need a way to remind them of expectations you've agreed to and then have a consistent response to the behavior that is not meeting expectations. We will delve into that later in the next chapter, but first let's finish exploring the traffic-light tool, specifically the behavioral choices represented by the yellow and red lights.

Yellow: Not Meeting Expectations

Yellow behavior choices violate the family expectations, take the child off course from accomplishing family hopes and dreams, but are not unsafe behaviors. Most undesirable behavior falls in this category. You *always* respond to yellow behavior choices with Redirection, the approach we will explore later.

consistent is also one of the hardest things we have to do. There are so many factors that contribute to how much energy we have for parenting. That's why having, and using, a system like Reset Families is so important. The structure provides you with the support you need to be consistent in your responses, allowing this to more easily become your default.

I'm sure that some of you are thinking this all sounds wonderful, but what happens if the child does not go to reset. We promise that we will address that issue, but before we go there we want to do a quick review of the entire redirection system and discuss the various choices our children may make and what our response should be.

Stop and Reflect:

What cues might work for you and your kids? What part of the Redirection System do you expect to be most challenging?

EXPECTATIONS AND REDIRECTION

Self-Management Repair Chart
Response to YELLOW behavior

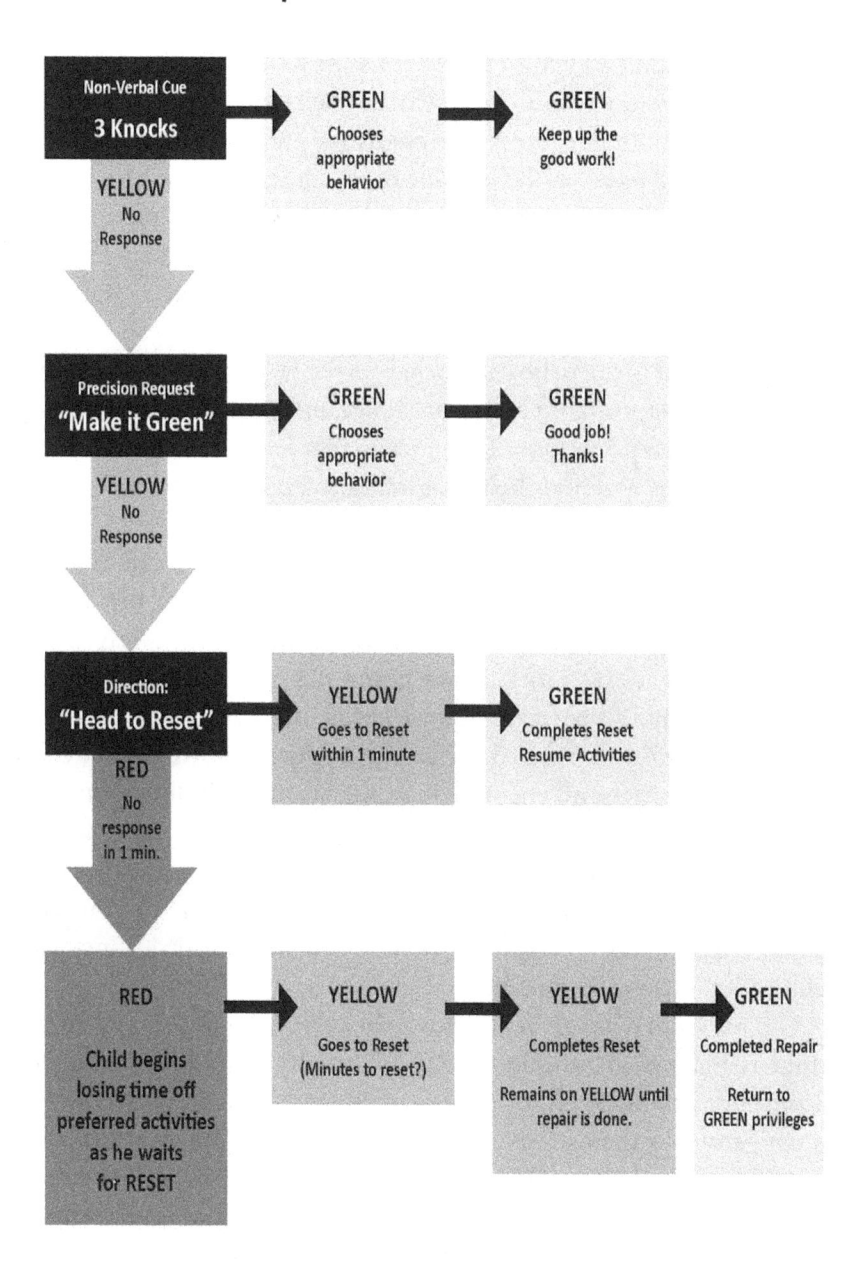

Non-Verbal Cue: 3 Knocks → **GREEN** Chooses appropriate behavior → **GREEN** Keep up the good work!

YELLOW No Response ↓

Precision Request: "Make it Green" → **GREEN** Chooses appropriate behavior → **GREEN** Good job! Thanks!

YELLOW No Response ↓

Direction: "Head to Reset" → **YELLOW** Goes to Reset within 1 minute → **GREEN** Completes Reset Resume Activities

RED No response in 1 min. ↓

RED Child begins losing time off preferred activities as he waits for RESET → **YELLOW** Goes to Reset (Minutes to reset?) → **YELLOW** Completes Reset Remains on YELLOW until repair is done. → **GREEN** Completed Repair Return to GREEN privileges

Let's use the Self-Management Repair Chart to review and expand on our knowledge of redirection, the process of stopping the undesired behavior, while teaching our children how to manage their own behavior.

The shading and color labels in the boxes are important and let you know how to respond to the various behavior choices your child makes. For a color version of this chart, visit www.resetfamilies.org.

The *black boxes* on the left side of the chart contain information about Redirection. They represent the steps in the redirection process. The shading and color labels in the rest of the boxes and arrows refer to the traffic-light system and give us information or the color of the child's choice and your response to that choice.

The light shaded boxes labeled *"green"* indicate that the child has made an appropriate behavior choice and is meeting or is taking steps to meet expectations. That means that they enjoy all the privileges associated with that behavior including praise, potential reward and unbroken relationship.

The shaded boxes and arrows labeled *"yellow"* indicate that the child is intentionally not meeting expectations. Yellow just means they have limited privileges. Try not to be punitive or overly tough during this time. It's more of not going out of your way. You may not be as likely to say yes as you would be if they were in the green zone behaviorally. During this time, it is important to remain calm and have a positive and encouraging tone when reminding them that you would love to help them as soon as they have made repair for the behavior choice that put them in the yellow zone. It is important to give them the opportunity to put their relationship with you back on the right track, by keeping the account short and dealing with restoration as soon as possible.

The shaded boxes and arrows labeled *"red"* indicate that the child is making an unsafe choice. They may be mildly defiant or downright oppositional, or they may be involved in an activity that is dangerous to themselves or others such as running into the street or hitting their brother. We never use the first two cues of the redirection system for red behaviors. The child is asked to go directly to reset. They may be so escalated or dangerous that they need your

EXPECTATIONS AND REDIRECTION

help to get there. Try not to be punitive in your tone and approach but you must engage directly at this time and take charge.

The important lesson we are teaching them in this process is that their choices do have consequences. If a child is on red, it means they have had the opportunity to accept responsibility and make a green choice, but they are choosing not to. They are not entitled to privileges at this time, and you should do nothing that requires anything extra from you. It is crucial at this point that they understand the severity of their choice, and they must complete reset if restoration is to occur. So until they have decided to make an effort toward meeting expectations and making repairs, as a parent you provide just the necessities of life—food, clothing, and shelter so to speak.

This is not easy to do. You will feel pressure from others to give in or lighten up. It's important to remember that even though your child may call you mean, you are not being mean. You have your child's best interest at heart. You are more concerned about their long-term success than their short-term happiness. And because you care so much for them, you have empowered them to make choices. Those choices have agreed upon consequences. Your child has the opportunity to turn their behavior around whenever they choose. Don't be punitive or hold a grudge. When they choose to take responsibility for their behavior choices and work toward making repairs, they are back on their way to green, or a restored relationship, and all the privileges that come with that. They are empowered. They are agents in their own lives, able to influence their reality by the choices they are making.

We will talk about the finer points and challenges of reset and what to do with the difficult situations, but your response to red behavior is always the same, you instruct them to head to reset in a calm but firm voice and intervene directly. We never use the first two cues of redirection in response to red behavior.

Now let's look back at the chart and the progression of choice a child may make. Refer to the black box on the left at the top of the chart:

Step 1 – Nonverbal Cue

Give the cue once, move on and continue what you are doing, giving them adequate time to make a positive choice. Do not engage in any discussion.

They have two choices at this point:

First, to the right of the black box, the first shaded box labeled *"Green"* indicates that they choose the appropriate green behavior. If they make this choice, move to the right to the second shaded box labeled *green* that indicates the response that you will give. Praise them specifically by saying something that ties the behavior to the family expectations like "Great work being responsible by picking up your toys and getting ready for dinner." They have returned to the green zone with restored relationship and no loss of privileges or the need for a lecture or additional consequences.

Second, below the nonverbal cue box the the shaded arrow labeled *yellow* indicates that they still have not changed the behavior. Maybe this choice is really challenging for your child. After you have waited a short time to give them the opportunity to comply and they ignore you or avoid making the change, they are still making a yellow behavior choice and it is time to move to step two and give the precision request.

Step Two – Precision Request (located in the second *black* box down the left side of the chart)

Give the cue "Make it green" once, move on, and continue what you are doing, giving them adequate time to make a positive choice. Do not engage in any discussion.

Again, they have two choices at this point:

First, moving to the shaded box labeled *green* on the right, they choose to comply and make the appropriate behavior choice. They are making a green choice and their actions return them to the green zone and the privileges associated with restored relationship. This box and the one next to it on the right are very important. Make sure you praise them by saying something like, "I know that was a tough choice for you. Thanks for choosing to be responsible by picking up your toys." Once again, there is no need for additional consequences or lectures. Really. This can be hard for some of us. Even though they've made the right choice, we feel the need to lecture them on how to do better next time. Instead, let's save our energy and attention for the positive behavior. They are beginning to manage their own behavior!

Second, below the Precision Request cue box the shaded arrow labeled *yellow* indicates that they still have not changed the behavior. Again, maybe this choice is really challenging for your child. After you have waited a short time to give them the opportunity to comply and they ignore you or avoid making the change, they are making a yellow behavior choice. You have waited patiently for a short time, and they just can't pull it together to make a good choice. They are still on yellow behavior. What do you do?

Step Three – Reset (located in the third black box down the left side of the chart)

Give the cue "Head to reset" once, move on, and continue what you are doing, giving them adequate time to make a positive choice. Give the instruction in a calm voice and move on. Do not engage in discussion at this time.

Remember, reset is the restorative part of redirection. They are not in trouble—it's not red behavior. It's not punitive. It's not "time out." Reset is an opportunity for the child to take time to reflect on their choice. This is that teaching moment where they have calmed down enough to consider their choices and to learn what they can do differently to meet the expectation.

Once again, they have two choices:

First, moving to the right of the *blue* box, the child is given one minute to reset. So for the purposes of our discussion at this point, they are compliant and have made their way to the reset location and are calming down. That is a green choice as indicated by the small arrow. However, following that arrow to the right, you see that the shaded box is labeled *yellow*, indicating that they are still on *yellow* behavior, with limited privileges until they have completed the reset sheet and the repair that is determined. Reset does not have to last a specific amount of time.

Second, after they have processed the event in a positive manner and have finished the reset sheet, they return to the green behavior zone, a restored relationship and the associated privileges. They have moved to the shaded box labeled *green* to the right. Remember to give them specific praise for making the right choice and making the repair they needed by completing the reset sheet. Reassure them of your love, and let them know that they are ready to move on. This can be hard for those of us who grow up being put on restriction. The focus of Reset Families is on teaching our kids that when we mess up we own our actions, make repairs, and move on. And isn't that how it works in our adult lives? When we mess up, we get stuck in the relational mess and consequences until we own our part and make repairs.

What if My Child Resists Reset?

Let's finish going through the Self-Management Repair Chart and see how we respond when our child is not ready to reset.

Referring to the shaded arrow labeled *red*, directly under the third black box on the left side of the chart, you can see that the child is not ready to comply. During your training sessions with your children, remind them that you are not going to argue with them, but when you give the instruction to "head to reset," you will set a timer and keep track of the time they take before going to reset. Reassure them that if they need more time to get to reset they can have it, but they will need to make up the time they took off their next preferred activity. Remain calm with an air of expectation in your voice. You are not angry. They have a choice and that choice comes with consequences. By their choice the child has moved down the left side of the chart to the bottom shaded box labeled "red".

The first few times you use the system you may need to give them a verbal cue such as "I see you're not ready to go to reset, I'll just set a timer and you can make up this time later." After a few times, they know the drill, so don't give the verbal cue, just look at your watch or the clock and go about your business—don't engage in any discussion. But what if you have given them the support they

EXPECTATIONS AND REDIRECTION

need and waited for one minute to give them time to make a positive choice and enter the reset process, but they are stubborn or just not ready to comply? (And that will happen.) What should you do now?

To the right of the shaded box labeled *red*, *you notice an arrow* pointing to the first shaded box labeled *yellow* box. You have waited for that teachable moment, and you can see the stubborn resolve melt away, and they have moved to reset. That is a green behavior choice as indicated by the arrow. They are being cooperative, have filled out the reset sheet with a positive attitude, or at least a willing attitude!

Now refer to the second shaded box labeled *yellow*. At this point, even though they made a green choice to complete reset and you have given them specific praise for making that choice, they will remain on yellow behavior, with limited privileges, until they have completed their "owed time." In addition, they must complete their repair by fixing the mess or damage they created by their choice before they return to green privileges. You are not angry or punitive, trying to lay guilt or shame on them; they are merely experiencing the result of their choice to be stubborn.

Finally, refer to the final shaded box labeled *green* on the bottom right. Once they have completed their "owed time" and the repair needed to fix the mess, they have restored the relationship and return to green-behavior privileges. This is time to celebrate with specific praise. Always end reset with an assurance of your love for them. It's nice to be reminded that we are loved, even when we've messed up.

What do you do when your child has been refusing to head to reset and you have someplace you need to be, or something you need to do? You move on, for the moment. But remember, the child is on red because they have not completed reset. This means if you go to Grandma's house, they have no privileges there either. Now, if they are ready, they can reset with you when you get to grandma's and begin to work on their repairs. But the bottom line is they are on red until they choose to complete reset.

If there is a situation where this absolutely can't work, like if you are dropping them off a daycare on your way to work, or they need to go to school, then you will pick up where you left off when you get home. The important thing is that you don't forget and always follow through with the reset process. Kids are smart. If they notice that if they hold out long enough they don't have to take responsibility for their actions or make repairs for their mistakes, they are going to hold out. If that happens and you neglect to get back to the reset process, you have reinforced their negative behavior, your relationship has taken a hit, and you have undermined the effectiveness of the approach.

The redirection system is purposefully designed to be simple and straightforward. Both you and your children can become experts. But just because the steps of the system are simple, doesn't mean it's easy to do. Kids are not simple, and all are different. It takes a lot of discipline to train our kids to be self-managers, and it takes a lot of discipline to train us to respond rather than react to our child's behavior. You have been practicing your current way of handling problems for a long time. It's reasonable to expect that you will have to practice this system before it starts to become a natural response.

I know that you have a lot of questions in your mind, and we're not going to leave you hear without answers to the tough challenges when you are met with resistance. We will spend more time in the next chapter talking about how to handle the very resistant child. But first, let's go back and unpack the characteristics of redirection. That will help us solidify the how with the why.

> **Stop and Reflect**
>
> Take time to talk yourself through the Self-Management Repair Chart.

The Characteristics and Purpose of Redirection

The purpose of redirection is not to punish our kids for their behavior choices but to help them take ownership of their behavior choices and become self-managers. It can be hard to make the transition from punishment to support in our heads and in our actions when our kids are misbehaving. But if we do, we will see a big difference in our interactions with them. Rather than fixing the problem with punishment, we respond to the child's mistakes as an opportunity for teaching them skills.

In review, let's take a look at some of the characteristics of redirection and the benefits we are likely to experience as we help our kids learn to manage their own behavior.

1. Redirection avoids nattering and power struggles.

Power struggles are common in parenting but very destructive to the parent-child relationship. Redirection provides an alternative to power struggles that helps us respond to our child's behavior with skills and support rather than reacting out of anger.

2. Redirection prevents reinforcing the undesired behavior.

Power struggles often result in frustration and simply giving up so that we can have a bit of peace and quiet. When we give in, we reinforce negative behavior and increase the likelihood that the child will persist in using negative behavior, thinking we are going to give in. We also miss the opportunity to help our child gain the skills they need to manage their own behavior. Besides damaging our relationship with the child, we miss the opportunity to empower our kids with the necessary skills they need in the individual situation but also in life as an adult.

3. Redirection is direct and unemotional.

When you implement redirection, you are mastering the skills to respond rather than react to your child's behaviors. Instead of flying off the handle and yelling, you are able to stop the behavior early, before it drives you crazy and draws you into a power struggle. Instead of finally giving in when you just can't stand the behavior any longer, you are able to consistently hold to the expectation. We don't mean to suggest that redirection is perfect or easy, it is neither, but whatever effort you make will take you closer to children becoming self-managers.

4. Redirection prevents playing one caregiver against the other.

By providing a consistent response to family expectations that are agreed on, all caregivers can respond to behavior in the same manner and support behavior change in the child. It works best when the system is shared and embraced by a spouse, partner, grandparent, or other caregivers. This book allows you to share your response to your children's' behavior with those providing care so that you can create a safe and consistent environment for your child.

5. Redirection builds consistency and predictability when expectations are clear.

When is the big question. Redirection does not work if the expectations are not clear. In the last chapter we learned the importance of clear expectations. We must teach and reteach the expectations during reset and through validation, reward, and reminders. Once the expectations are clear, and we consistently use the redirection system, kids are empowered to make choices because they can predict what will happen. It's not a game of chance for the child to see if they will get away with something. You have the tools in place to be consistent, and consistency on your part encourages your kids to self-manage.

This chapter has been full of "if this occurs," then "that will likely happen," but the reset process is really about creating a consistent response. With practice, this system will empower you and your kids to work together toward achieving your family vision.

EXPECTATIONS AND REDIRECTION

Putting Reset Families into Practice:

You may notice that "in Five Minutes or Less" is missing from the title. Teaching your kids the redirection system will take time. It is important that they understand how it will work and have input on the process before you launch into using it.

Hopefully by now, you have done the following:

- Moving forward, these can be reinforced in five minutes or less, so keep it up!
- Work together to create a project that reminds you of your family vision.
- Look for the positive behavior and reward it with specific, authentic praise.
- Notice what triggers your child. When they seem to be overwhelmed and frustrated, use "take a break."
- Brainstormed family rules and clarified your Reset Families Expectations.

Training for Redirection:

- Review the traffic-light system and how that is connected to expectations
- Remind them that redirection is only used when they are choosing yellow behavior.
- Introduce the three cues and watch the video together.
- Decide together what the nonverbal and precision cues will be.
- Have the children role play the system, with you being the child and them giving the cues. It makes it more fun! Use the Practice Scenarios (pg. 183)
- Begin to use the first two cues as reminders for them to manage their own behavior when they are not meeting expectations.

Further Resources, Page 183

CHAPTER 6

Focus on Restoration – Using Reset Effectively

In the last chapter we crossed over the line from the philosophical and foundational aspects of Reset Families to the practical and tangible "how to" of redirection, the behavior management approach. Hopefully you have been spending time on the foundational pieces, like looking at areas of growth in your own life, creating a shared family vision, learning to spend time together strengthening family connections, and setting clear expectations. It is during this time that you are creating the family culture needed to support the behavior-management system.

Without the work we have been asking you to do on the foundational pieces to strengthen your family relationships, the redirection system will be mildly effective at best. Relationship is the beginning of any effective discipline. Kids have to know that you value them, that you think they are worthy of your time. They need to know that you are hopeful about who they are and their ability to manage their own behavior. They have to know that you're on their side, supporting them as they build the skills to do just that.

The real impact to your family comes as you balance the value of relationships with self-management and accountability. The reset step in redirection is designed to help you find that balance. There is both accountability for behaviors and value placed on relationship when you are able to take time with your child after the frustration and storm of a behavior challenge is over. During reset you help them reflect, take ownership of their action, make a better plan for the future, and most importantly, repair the damage done by their behavior choice, so that they can move on with restored relationship.

It is so easy to become tangled in a tug-of-war between relationship and accountability. There are times as parents that we are drawn into a conflict, and then we dig in our heels as we hand out punishment with increasing severity until our child finally submits to our demands. We walk away satisfied they have complied with our wishes but frustrated and discouraged by the relationship that was sacrificed in the name of getting the homework done or the teeth brushed.

At other times, we want so badly for our kids to be happy, or to like us, that we prevent natural consequences by rescuing them, or we go back on consequences that have previously been agreed on. When we do that, we inadvertently encourage our kids to play the odds. They believe there is a good chance they might get away with whatever they are tempted to do that they already know they shouldn't, so they take the risk. When we believe we have to choose between holding our kids accountable *or* having a strong relationship, we often find ourselves being inconsistent in our parenting. Inconsistent parenting leads to frustration, confusion, and loss of relationship quality for everyone in the family. Our attempt to make everyone happy all the time leads to no one being happy most of the time. We don't have to choose. We can hold our kids accountable *and* build a strong relationship. It's not always easy, and they may not thank you for it right away, but it is possible. The Reset Families tools can help you do just that.

Purpose of Reset

Restorative justice emphasizes the importance of repairing the harm caused by one's behavior rather than a focus on retribution or punishment. The reset process not only helps kids understand that they can repair the damage they have caused but teaches them how so they can move on. The caregiver's job during reset is to help the child reflect on the behavior choice made, how it violated family expectations, how the child could make a better choice in the future and repair any damage done. During the process caregivers help the child gain insight into their actions, feel empathy for others and learn how to make repair.

In line with the notion of restorative justice, let's think about the way we approach reset with our kids. The way you approach reset sets the tone with your child. It is important they know that they are not in trouble. Remember, redirection is comprised of three reminders, with reset being the third one. If we say reset is one more opportunity to manage behavior, but our tone of voice and body language says, "You're in big trouble, Mister," we are sending mixed messages.

This is not a time for punishment, rather, a time to reflect, have the child own their behavior, make repair, and move on. It would be easy to punish and move on, but that takes the child's control away and implies that she is a victim of your anger. When the focus is on their behavior choice, it is easier for the child to see that reset and the repairs you decide on are the direct result of their behavior choice and their inability to manage their own behavior. This means the children learn that they are agents in their own lives. Their actions can have a direct impact on their reality.

Reset gives the children one more chance to reflect on their choices and manage that behavior. Remember the premise of Reset Families is that they are strong and smart and that they can manage their behavior. And frankly they would probably rather manage it themselves than having you manage it for them. Not many children like to be told what to do all the time.

Reset also provides time for the child to examine and own the behavior choices. They do this by reflecting on the damage that was done and by identifying the repair that is needed in order to make things right or restore the relationship. The questions on the reset sheet take them through the steps to help them achieve restoration. Rather than a "you do the crime, you do the time" mentality, reset encourages kids to focus on restoration. Let's face it, we're all going to blow it from time to time. The question is not if, but when. That's why we want to empower our kids with the skills to make repairs when they do. When they realize they can make repairs, they understand that they do not have to be defined by the mistakes they make.

They are empowered to restore the situation and the relationship and then start again.

If my husband forgets that it's date night and works late, leaving me all dressed up with no place to go, what do I want from him? Do I want him to come home and take his punishment like a man, until I decide he's learned his lesson? Not really. What I want is for him to recognize and own his mistake and then work at repairing the damage that was done. Being able to take the punishment is not nearly as restorative as being willing to make the repairs. The other side of that is that I have to be open to forgiving and restoring, rather than labeling him by that particular behavior.

Or how about if a coworker completely misses a deadline, fails to communicate, and gets the whole team reprimanded? What do I want from that coworker? I want them to take responsibility, apologize to the team, and then work hard to complete the work as soon as possible so we can move forward as a team.

The restoration process in reset teaches our children skills for life and that relationships are worth the effort. They cannot be perfect. They won't always be able to avoid failure, mistakes, or even poor choices, but they can gain the skills to navigate those setbacks in ways that will build character, strengthen relationships, and lead to restoration.

Beyond just repairing the damage, we also hope that people in our lives will have a change of heart, so that next time they are tempted to make choices that negatively impact themselves or others, they will make a better choice instead. The process of reset provides a pattern for restoration that is likely to result in heart change. We have all been around people who vent their anger and frustration, get it off their chests, and believe that is the end of it. Unfortunately, they may think it is over and done with, but in reality, it is festering beneath the surface, and resentment begins to build in the relationship.

Reset helps you begin developing that skill right now, hopefully when your kids are young. We don't want just a quick fix that stops the behavior, although that is certainly helpful in the moment. What we want to see is gradual movement toward an attitude and heart change in our child. We want to see change that allows them to imagine what the other person is feeling and to develop empathy toward them. We want to help our children reflect on their inner thoughts and feelings rather than feeling a lack of worth. They are empowered to repair the damage and move on.

Rather than seeing themselves as a victim of circumstances or another person's anger, we want to help our kids realize the power they have to be agents in their own lives. We want to help them gain skills that empower them to manage their behavior, and when they are not successful, to embrace an attitude that is eager to seek restoration. The attitude change is most likely when our kids feel safe and know that we have their backs. When they know that while we may be frustrated with their behavior, we believe that they are greater than that mistake and that we trust them to fix it and move on. When the behavior is labeled rather than making them feel judged or punished, it creates an atmosphere of hope where they can develop an attitude of restoration.

That movement is likely to happen during reset when you take them back to your values and expectations. When you identified your hopes and dreams together, what expectations did you all agree would move you closer to that family vision? How did their behavior move them away from that vision? How can they dig deep and gain the strength to make the change they need, and many times want to make? By helping them take ownership of their behavior choices, you are on track to help them be accountable for their choices but realize that they can repair and gain skills to restore the relationship.

Reset is a time to ask them about the character traits they will need to develop to reach their goals but is not a time for lecture. Keep it short and simple. The more you talk, the less value your words carry. When you talk too much, most kids ultimately shut down and just wait for the noise to stop. As the kids get a bit older and are dealing with issues of strength and faith, ask them questions about how their values or faith help them to make difficult life changes. When the time is right and they express interest in hearing about how it worked when you were a kid, you may share about your source of strength and a time you experienced restoration after a challenging interaction.

USING RESET EFFECTIVELY

Sometimes our kids get the impression that life was easier for us. In some ways, it was. At least we didn't have to worry about our picture being spread all over social media or the possibility of a school shooting. But we all know we have faced challenges in life where we made choices that either led to positive outcomes or negative outcomes. At age appropriate levels, we believe it's important to share your successes and failures with your children. It's likely to give them hope that they can make changes too, even if it's hard.

> **Stop and Reflect**
>
> Where do you get the motivation to change when something is difficult? What bigger picture or greater good drives you? What drives or motivates your kids and how is that different than you expected?

There are so many benefits to utilizing the reset process in your family. When you are tired, or it feels too time consuming, or you're tempted to go back to your default parenting style, remember that reset allows you to provide accountability and build relationship. It teaches a pattern for owning mistakes and making repairs . . . Reset also gives you an opportunity to connect, even around mistakes, to reflect on the family values and have conversations that lead to heart-change. Finally, when used consistently with a focus on restoration and moving on, reset builds the likelihood of your child being compliant to future requests. Besides the heart and attitude change, your kids will gradually begin to be motivated internally and "choose" to be compliant by managing their behavior. That just sounds a lot more hopeful and purposeful than simply grounding them for a day or a week. So let's go back to the "how-to" part of setting up Reset for success.

1. **Determine your reset location in advance.**
At home, reset should always happen in the same location. When choosing a reset location, be sure to choose someplace that's free from toys, clutter, and distractions, where children can process

their choice and come up with a plan for success. At home it might be at the end of the hall on a beanbag, away from other family activity, but where they can see what is going on. That may give them a sense of urgency to complete the reset so that they can return to the family activity. Some people have a place where they can store reset sheets or a journal and pens in or near the reset location.

Houses come in all shapes and sizes, with all kinds of layouts. Think about your home. Do you have someplace where you can't see the TV? A place where you might easily happen by, perhaps the bottom of the stairs, in a hallway, or by the front door? If you have more than one child, you may want to come up with a backup reset location. It is possible that more than one of your kids needs to go to reset at the same time.

When you are away from home, discuss the reset plan as you are traveling to the event before a problem occurs. For example, at the grocery store, reset may be at the shopping cart. You may something like "If you cannot manage your behavior I will ask you to reset with your hand on the shopping cart until we leave the store and can complete the reset process. You may not leave the cart until we are finished shopping." Then when you get to the car or back home you need to return to the process and have them complete the reset sheet. Some people have a laminated Reset sheet in the car with an erasable marker so that they can process away from home.

2. **Make certain that your child knows what is expected at reset in advance.**

When you have asked them to head to reset, that is not the time to have to communicate the procedure. You don't want to engage verbally at this point. They should be able to head to reset and know exactly what they are supposed to be doing. Make sure they know where to go, what they are to do, and how they are to behave. You may say, "The first thing you need to do when you get to reset, it to take three deep breaths and calm down. I will know that you are ready to reset when you are sitting on the beanbag with a calm body and your voice is off. Then I will ask you to take the time to think about your choice and fill in the reset sheet. When you have finished

USING RESET EFFECTIVELY

that, I will come back, and we will go over it together quickly so you can return to your activity."

Remember, this is not a conversation you have after you send them to reset. You want the kids to know how it's going to work before they need to use it. A fun way to practice is role-play with you as the kid who needs to go to reset. Let your kids take turns sending you to reset. Show them what appropriate reset behavior is, and maybe, for the fun of it, model what you don't want to see. If you have a laminated sheet and easy erase pen in the reset location, they can start the process as soon as they are ready. If you don't have a laminated reset sheet available at the location, you will need to make sure you notice right away when they are ready, and hand them a reset sheet to complete. When they are still escalated they are likely to wad up a paper reset sheet and toss it, giving you one more challenge to deal with.

It is very difficult for some children to sit quietly. They may need to be able to walk around, pace, or have a squishy ball to expend some of their energy. But they need to know the boundaries of the area they are required to stay in, and the accompanying behavior you expect needs to be very clearly defined. Again, modeling the behavior, before it's needed, is a great way to make sure the expectations are clear. It can be easy to get dragged into a power struggle or resort to nagging as you wait for your child to be ready to complete reset. The clearer the expectations are in the beginning, the less likely you are to get drawn into a negative exchange.

3. Use a calm voice and body language to instruct your child to head to reset.

The way you approach reset, hopefully with a calm voice and body language, is critically important. Your attitude and actions reassure your child that they are not in trouble but that they have to make a change. Your instruction and attitude need to be filled with empathy and hope of restoration rather than fear and rejection. If you are tense and shouting at them to "get to reset" you have effectively communicated that they are in trouble. Your attitude and approach can either set the tone for restoration or build walls that undermine your relationship.

Be sure to give the instruction *only* once, and then move on. When their body is calm and they are meeting your expectations for the reset process, hand them a reset sheet or instruct them to take it from the folder near the reset location. Be sure to check back often, but subtly, so you can catch them quickly when they have finished the reset sheet and are ready for reflection and repair.

4. **Review the form with your child.**
If they have answered the questions seriously, with enough effort, briefly talk through the answers, and figure out the repair. This is not the time to demand complete sentences or to worry about proper punctuation. Ask them if they are ready to make a good choice. When they agree they can do that, thank them for taking responsibility for their actions and remind them of how much you love them.

Let's take a moment to review the Reset Reflection Sheet point by point.

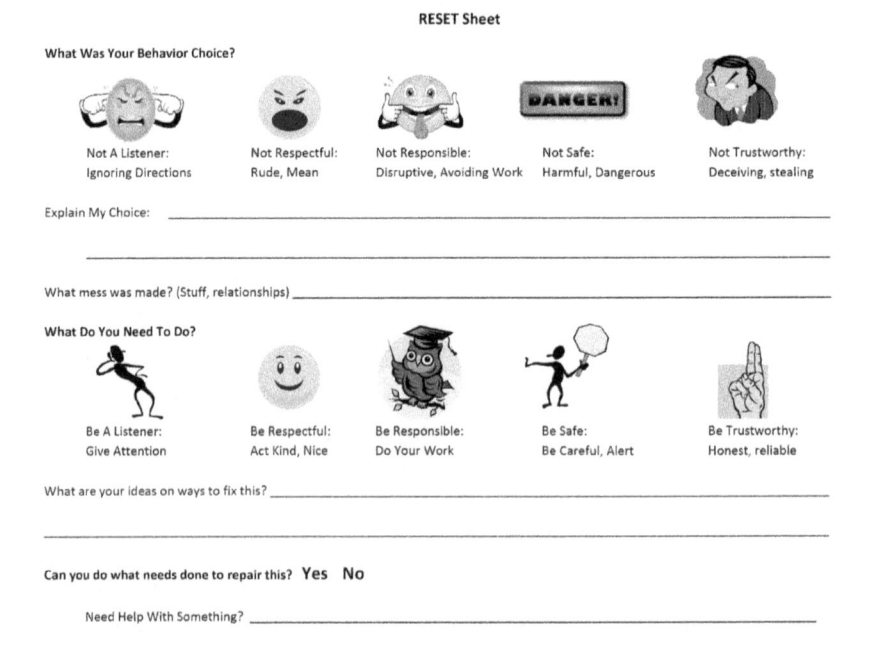

RESET Sheet

What Was Your Behavior Choice?

| Not A Listener: Ignoring Directions | Not Respectful: Rude, Mean | Not Responsible: Disruptive, Avoiding Work | Not Safe: Harmful, Dangerous | Not Trustworthy: Deceiving, stealing |

Explain My Choice: _____

_____

What mess was made? (Stuff, relationships) _____

What Do You Need To Do?

| Be A Listener: Give Attention | Be Respectful: Act Kind, Nice | Be Responsible: Do Your Work | Be Safe: Be Careful, Alert | Be Trustworthy: Honest, reliable |

What are your ideas on ways to fix this? _____

_____

Can you do what needs done to repair this? Yes   No

Need Help With Something? _____

USING RESET EFFECTIVELY

What was your behavior choice?

The child can circle the appropriate icon representing the expectation they were not meeting. Most children age five and above can figure out the response to the first question. Then depending on their age and personality they may prefer that you talk it through with them rather than requiring them to write out the answers. The important thing is that they reflect, and if they can reflect better with your support, work with them and make it a teaching moment.

If working together quickly spirals into arguing, blaming, or excuse making, gently remind them they are thinking about their own choices, and if necessary, give them a bit more time to reflect alone. You are ready to process reset when both you, and the child, can talk about the situation without becoming highly agitated. If you're not ready, it is better to set them free from Reset and let them know when you will be coming back together to talk about it. Step one is meant to be simple. If they say, "I wasn't being a listener," but you feel you sent them to reset for not being responsible, validate their response and suggest your idea in addition. You might say, "True, you didn't listen when I asked you to clear your plate, which also means you weren't being responsible."

What happened?

You have been avoiding interaction up to this point. With the first two cues, you gave the cue and then walked away making sure not to engage. That is what prevents the power struggles and allows both of you to calm down and be ready to reflect and process the incident. Now it is time to give your child voice and the opportunity to tell you what happened. You most likely didn't see the whole episode unfold, and a sibling may have been teasing the child and that is what prompted their angry words or actions. You may find out that you have another child who needs to reset as well. Reassure the child that you will deal with their sibling, but that for now, you will focus on their actions.

You may have seen the whole thing, but you don't know what was going on in their inner world. What is frustrating them, or what was their perspective on the situation? This question, "What happened?" is an opportunity for your child to be heard. It is important that this is part of reset. When we consistently give our kids voice to share their side of the story in reset, they begin to trust that they will be heard. Then, they are more able to go to reset without arguing because they know they'll have a chance to explain themselves. Be sure to give them that chance, and try not to interrupt other than to ask clarifying questions.

It is more important to have them tell you what happened rather than asking them to explain why they did it. Often, they simply don't know why. Their answer to this question will help you make sure you see it from their perspective and will help you come up with appropriate repair. Occasionally a child may get reminders and earn a reset with absolutely no idea why he was asked to head to reset. If he doesn't know what he did wrong, ask him to try and remember or simply tell him what you saw or what was reported to you. If he can't come up with the answer just tell him rather than get into an argument. You are asking them so you can see the situation from their perspective.

What damage was done to stuff or to relationships?

If the child got angry and made a big mess by throwing the color crayons across the room, it is fairly easy for them to figure out the damage that was done. There is a big mess in the room and maybe some broken crayons that need to be cleaned up. If on the other hand they called their sibling a name they need to think about the relational damage that was done. It may be hard for them to verbalize the damage done to relationships. You can help by asking them questions such as "How do you think they felt?" or "Did you like how that went?" "What do you think your sister thought?" What you really want to help your child do is to put themselves in the other person's shoes, and since they have had the opportunity to tell their side of the story, they will more likely be able to be empathic.

USING RESET EFFECTIVELY

What should I do next time?

This is another simple opportunity to circle the characteristic they want to exhibit instead. If they weren't a listener in question one, then in this question they would circle "Be a listener." But this can also be a chance to build skills. This question presents a great opportunity to ask them to come up with ideas so that they can avoid this type of thing happening again. You may want to review "take a break" or come up with suggestions of ways to make a better choice such as "walk away" or "ask them to stop." If they have no ideas, it is beneficial to come up with some suggestions and ask them to pick from the ideas. This is the time to help them add a few tools to their relational tool belt. When they are the ones to choose the options, it teaches them to sift through ideas for something that will work for them.

How can you fix this?

Allow them ample time to come up with their own suggestions of repair first. Cleaning up a mess they made is simple and straightforward and all that may be needed. However, when there are relational issues, they need time to think through the repair. Sometimes they may even come up with a repair that seems excessive to us. Their sense of justice may require more than what we might expect so it is good to reinforce their ability to come up with appropriate repair. When we suggest something that seems "too easy" or "too light," we have undermined the seriousness of the event for them and restoration does not feel as complete for them. However, if they have suggested a repair that is extreme, it is a good time to help them be realistic about the damage that was done and how much it actually takes to make repair.

Sometimes it may be necessary to ask the person who was hurt in the situation to offer suggestions for repairs. My (Angel) five-year-old likes to fix everything with a hug. We validate that response, if the person who was hurt would like a hug. But, if it's her eleven-year-old foster brothers, that's not so much a repair; in fact, it may feel like further damage. In that case we encourage her to think what the other person might like. If a hug is a good start, then we will say, "Yes, a hug is a good start, what else?" This is the most empowering part of reset. It's at this point that we turn the corner from a focus on what we did wrong, to hope for the future. We are now focused on what we can do to make the situation right and move forward.

Do you need help to fix this? Yes or no?

Simply ask them to circle their choice. They may need help reaching the cleaner, going to the store, or holding the dustpan. They may not be able to fix something they break like a broken window or a hole in the wall, so this is the place to figure out what their part will be in making repairs. They may need to help dad or mom with some of their chores when they are fixing the mess, or they may need to work to help pay for the repair. We will discuss this more in the chapter on consequences.

Can you do what we agreed on to fix this?

With this question, you are checking to make sure they are ready to comply. Don't skip this question. Sometimes the transition from thinking about repairs to doing them is a tough one. By asking them this question, they aren't surprised when reset is done and they need to go actually do the repair.

> **Stop and Reflect:**
>
> Review the reset sheet. Which part do you believe will be most difficult for your child? How can you encourage them through the difficult places?

Dealing with Resistance to Reset

I wish I could say that, whenever you get to the third step of redirection, your child will suddenly realize the error of their ways, regulate their emotions, and head straight to reset without resistance. Unfortunately, that's not the case. There are times, when children refuse to go to reset. When you send your child to reset and they refuse, you are at a crossroads. This is where we have to be careful, and remember, we set the tone for our family. It is very easy to go back to the default of using power or simply giving in to get rid of the tension.

However, you have the tools now to make this a teaching time rather than a destructive power struggle. Reset gives you the opportunity to make an emotional connection with your child if your attitude and approach reassure them that you are not angry and that you believe they can fix their mistake and move on. That connection is the beginning of effective discipline and it requires intentionality. When handled properly, even a child's defiance can be an opportunity to teach them that they can be agents in their lives, capable of making choices that bring about consequences, positive and negative.

As we approach resistance to reset, it is very important to be consistent without becoming rigid. This means that we need to work from expectations and the values that we have developed based on our shared family vision. It is intentional parenting rather than falling back into our default parenting approach. You don't have to sacrifice relationships in order to enforce the expectations. You don't have to throw out the expectations in order to maintain relationship. When we become too rigid, the relationship suffers, but when we're too flexible, accountability and their respect for you go out the window. Effective parenting relies on both relationship and accountability.

After you have taken some time to get used to the Reset Families model, if your kids are frequently resistant to reset, consider whether you are being as consistent as you can be. We have all helped develop the curriculum and write this book. We've been teaching Reset Families for years. We've used the Reset Families model in our homes and various other settings. Nevertheless, we constantly fall off the wagon of being consistent. It happens when we get too tired or too busy. It also happens when we are having lots of fun like on vacations, holidays, and summer breaks.

The Reset Families model begins with the recognition that change in our home begins with us. If something isn't working, a great place to look first is at ourselves. It is much easier to be consistent when our kids know the expectations we have set as a family, and when they can trust us to respond predictably when they are not meeting those expectations. Ask yourself if you've been praising the behavior you want to see. Have you found ways to celebrate when your kids are meeting expectations, in order to reinforce the expectations of the family?

Redirection, our response to yellow behavior, is a very structured response to behavior that falls short of our family expectations. When used to address that behavior every time, or realistically, most of the time, we set up a very predictable and safe environment for our kids.

Even with all your hard work of reinforcing the desired behavior, and being consistent, and all the support of reminders and opportunities to make the right choice, there are times when your child will refuse to go to reset. Knowing the importance of restoration, what can you do to prepare for those times? As much as we would like to avoid this situation and are frustrated and disappointed when our child cannot reset, we need to plan for reset resistance in advance. That way we are not caught off guard and resort back to nagging, yelling, heaping on consequences, or just giving up.

An ancient saying reminds us as parents not to come down too hard on our children, or we will crush them. It suggests that we take them by the hand and lead them. That's certainly our experience. When we are inconsiderate and harsh in our response to resistance, children often become exasperated and angry and feel like victims rather than agents in their lives. There is difference between rigid rule following that discourages and disempowers our children and loving accountability.

USING RESET EFFECTIVELY

Here are five things you can do to make reset more effective in the face of resistance. Let's look at each one of these separately:

1. **Enlist the child's help as you teach the reset system.**

As you teach reset, remind your child of the part they have played in creating your shared family vision, the family expectations, and coming up with the reminder cues. You may say something like, "We have agreed on the values that are important to us as a family. We also agreed that you would rather manage your own behavior instead of having us do that for you. Now we need to think about what will happen if there is ever a time that you choose not to manage your own behavior and refuse to go to reset."

Ask your child what they believe would be a fair consequence if they were to choose not to go to reset. When not in the moment, they are usually harder on themselves than you would be. But it's important to respect that feeling and what they have to say because it reflects their sense of justice. If they feel that it takes more than you think to "repair" for refusing to reset, honor that within reason.

Let them know that, when they finally head to reset, you will use the consequence you both have agreed on for their defiance and for all the time they chose not to engage. With the plan already in place you are halfway there—they have agreed on the consequence for refusing, and now they experience the reality of not only their choice, but also their agreed-on repair. Additional repairs may be necessary depending on the magnitude of their behavior, but we will discuss that in the next chapter when we think about consequences.

Signed contracts are good. When it is decided together and agreed on in advance, they have more buy-in, and when the moment of refusal comes, they are not the victim or your anger; it was a choice they made, and the repair is already decided. This does not necessarily mean they are going to like it. But with a plan in place, you are less likely to dish out unreasonable consequences that add to your child's frustration. And when the dust settles and cooler heads prevail, your child is likely to be able to see that the consequences were the result of their choices, rather than your wrath.

2. Be willing to wait for reset—meet resistance with patience.
Wait patiently with a positive attitude. That's the hard part. The child has now chosen to move to the red-behavior zone by refusing to move to reset within the allowed one minute. By waiting, you are not letting them off the hook. They will have to complete the reset process, but you are allowing time to take a break and deescalate. You are meeting resistance with patience, so wait for them to comply. It's so easy to get drawn into a power struggle, but if we plan in advance and allow time to wait patiently, then we are less likely to be drawn in and escalate the situation.

Remember, you are not angry. You remain positive in your approach, and you give your child the space they may need to process reset. You have set the timer and are keeping track of time they use before moving to reset. As the minutes stack up, you may remind them that they will begin to lose time off a preferred activity as you are waiting for them to go to reset. You may say something like, "I know this is really hard for you. You can take the time you need to calm down and make a good choice. You can make this time up later."

By waiting you increase the possibility of making an emotional connection with your child that is essential if you are going to have a teachable moment. Waiting also gives you both time to cool down and reflect. You have been practicing this with "take a break," and that approach fits here as well. You want to be able to control your emotions and let your child learn to do the same.

Waiting for that teachable moment allows reset to serve its purpose by providing a chance to reteach the behavior expectations in a guided conversation rather than a lecture. A teachable moment reinforces the skills they need to have in order to manage their behavior successfully. It will also allow time to help you determine the repair needed. Without that connection, it is easy to become rigid, going after the solution to the behavior in a punitive way. You may have temporarily stopped the behavior, but you have also planted the seeds of resentment rather than fostering relationship and restoration through a teachable moment.

Forcing compliance gets in the way of restoration. Sometimes when you rush reset, your child will comply with a bad attitude fed

USING RESET EFFECTIVELY

by anger and resentment. If your child is complying on the outside by sitting quietly, but they are standing up on the inside with a stubborn heart and mind, there is little room for change. Anger and resistance will prevent restoration.

Once the child has complied, even if it is reluctantly, it is important to reassure them by your actions that they can make repair and move on. Approaching them with anger, bitterness, or resentment will undermine the effectiveness of making the right choice and heading to reset. If our philosophy says, "Everyone makes mistakes, you are not defined by your mistakes, but by how you learn from and fix this," but we respond in our tone, actions, and body language with harshness, our kids will have a hard time going to reset. When we respond in a harsh way, Reset becomes a place of shame rather than a place of hope and restoration.

After you have outlined a plan for success in the future, decided together on the repair, and the child has complied, that is the time for reassurance. You may say something like "You really did some hard work fixing the mess you made by refusing to reset. I feel like you have owned your part in the problem and are working toward making the necessary repair. Yesterday, while you were very angry, you asked me to help you with a project in your bedroom. Why don't we go and do that now?" That action communicates that you are not angry and that they can actually move on without a cloud hanging over them for hours or days.

Once you have navigated through a stubborn refusal with your child, and they have paid the time back that they owe for failing to go to reset, you are ready to consider what they need to do to rebuild trust that has been broken. If they don't know exactly what they need to do to make repair and how long it will take, they will lose hope and quit trying. You may say, "When you are able to manage your behavior with the two reminders for one whole day, I will know you are ready to be a self-manager and you can have your iPad back again." The length of time and what you expect will be dependent on the magnitude of the misbehavior. We will discuss that more fully in the next chapter.

3. **Take time to listen and clarify.**

Occasionally, a child will be stubborn and hold out because they are confused about what they did or they feel the Reset if unfair. Remember, until this time you have not engaged in any discussion with the child, so you have not heard from their perspective. Let your child do the talking, rather than lecturing them. You are trying to understand what happened and there may be a simple solution.

Sometimes, once the clarification is made, they may be ready right then to do what you were asking in the first place, and there may be no need for additional repair. There is no need for further discussion. They just needed clarification. You are all ready to move on. In this situation, they may need a bit of additional training. Remind them that even if they don't understand or believe that the three knocks are given fairly, that they need to trust that you will allow them to clarify in reset. So rather than holding out, it is best to head to reset directly, so you can get it all figured out together. It may also be a good idea to teach them that they can have a voice and say as soon as you give them the nonverbal cue, "I will do what you ask, but I need you to listen to my side of the story."

The redirection system works very well when used consistently, but that doesn't mean that you will not experience situations that are challenging and you may miscommunicate. As you listen carefully and give your kids a chance to express their opinions, expecting and hoping for the best, you will build relationship and trust. These are the times when it is best to apologize for the misunderstanding, thank them for trusting you to be fair and move on without additional consequences.

4. **Understand the "why" of the behavior.**

Reset is where repair and consequences begin, and it is almost always helpful to clarify and understand the *why* of the behavior. Don't ask your child; they seldom know why, even when they can tell you the what. Focus with your child on what happened. During the reset process, you are looking for the why—the trigger, the event that led to the resistance. That is your job as the parent. Understanding

USING RESET EFFECTIVELY

the motive will also help you determine what repair might be appropriate and to help the child come up with a plan for future success.

When deciding on repairs consider the following motives that may have influenced their action:

Mistake (or Miscommunication)

Your child just forgot what they were supposed to be doing or was unclear about how meeting the expectation looks in a particular setting. For example, you may have company over and you tell our child to clean up before dinner. But you were not clear about how soon and what that really means. Does it mean "pick up the toys," "wash your hands," and "come and help set the table"?

During reset, it is much easier once you understand that it was lack of clear communication on your part, to clarify the expectation and allow them to follow up and move on. No lectures, extensive repairs, or drawn-out discussions are needed!

Mischief

This is a situation where your child knows the expectation but gave in to temptation or peer pressure. In this case, they know what is right to do, but they don't really know how to tell their friend no, or it just looks too enticing to pass up. For example, you may get busy and distracted when you have friends over. Your child knows that they are not supposed to have candy before dinner, but the jar is sitting there, and you notice that they have opened the jar and are helping themselves.

If you take time to think before you react, you will have a teachable moment. Otherwise, it escalates into anger and frustration, and you might be tempted to give repair that is beyond what is needed. In a situation like this you may give them the nonverbal cue, and they may respond by putting the candy back. There is no need for a big discussion then, because they turned it around.

However, don't miss the opportunity after guests are gone to talk about what to do when you are tempted to do something you know you shouldn't do. Same thing with peer pressure: if they understand the importance of making good choices, even when it is hard, that discussion is far more powerful than harsh consequences. Consequences or repairs may be necessary, but consider the severity of the choice. Always go back to the idea of repairs. What needs to be done to fix this? This is in contrast to "What can I do to make him miserable, so he'll never do that again?"

Mayhem

There are two types of mayhem: blatant defiance and red behavior. Blatant defiance is when the child knows the expectation but remains unwilling to follow it. There are not caught up in the moment; they are willingly and intentionally violating family expectations. In this case, you have given the reminders and asked the child to head to reset. As you process reset and consider the repairs, it will be important to include repairs for the relational damage or trust that is broken as a result of their defiant behavior choices.

Realizing that there are different motivations for our children's behavior choices helps us understand how to respond. Are they confused? We need to listen, provide clarity, and allow them to go get it right. Are they tempted? We want to encourage them to make repairs and help them gain the skills to resist temptation in the future. Is it mayhem? We want to intervene with kind but firm authority. In this case, safety is the priority, and repairs will almost always include repairing relational damage or broken trust in addition to the following through with meeting the original expectation.

Reset for red behavior

In the case where they are totally out of control, oppositional, or unsafe they are engaging in red behavior. This is the time for action. We don't use the three steps of redirection at this time. It is time to manage their behavior for them! We need to make certain that they are in a safe place and that we can keep others safe before we try to have a conversation. Once we have ensured safety, the child is sent directly to reset. The important thing is that we remember to consistently send them to reset once the situation is stabilized. It may be tempting to heave a sigh of relief after the danger has passed and forget to complete the reset process with them. It will take time, and you will most likely have to wait for the child, and you, for that matter, to be calm enough to process reset together. Repair is based on the severity of the event.

5. Be consistent but remain flexible.

When things are not working well, it is easy to become rigid, forcing a rule and issuing consequences without considering the child and the circumstances that led up to this resistance. As we have said before, every child is different and no approach, even when used consistently will work every time.

Here is where it is important to balance relationship with accountability. During Reset you want to communicate that your relationship with them is important and that they are worth the effort to work through this together to reach restoration. However, it is crucial at this crossroads that the child understands that they must complete reset and make repair in order to experience restoration to return to the green behavior zone with the associated privileges. That's how they understand that accountability for their behavior choice is part of repair and restoration.

Thinking back to the Self-Management Repair Chart on page 5, the child is in the red behavior zone until reset is complete with limited privileges. During this time, you meet their resistance with patience, making sure that there is no spirit of punishment in your approach. This is not a time for revenge but a gentle and persistent reminder that they need to make repair before they can move on. So you will need a response to your child's request to do something special before they have completed reset. You would respond by saying something like, "I would love to do this for you, but we have some repair to do first. So let me know when you are ready to finish reset."

During the time of the child's resistance, remain positive and tune in to your child watching for a softening in their attitude. Expect them to turn their attitude around, and do your part to look for the positive and encourage hope. This attitude reassures them that you will be there for them in the good times and the challenging ones as well.

Flexibility at a time like this may involve joining them and initiating conversation without initially requiring them to "go to the reset" location. It would be easy to build a wall with a very obstinate child by demanding compliance in a rigid way. They have to do the heart work in order for restoration to occur, but you can allow flexibility. You may say something like, "I really want you to be a self-manager, but if you don't choose to manage your own behavior, you won't be able to have the freedom and power that gives you. Refusing to go to reset is letting me know that you are not willing to manage your own behavior. I want to hear what happened. Can we both go to reset and talk about that?"

They may believe that they didn't deserve reset and to comply by going to the reset location at this point is just too difficult for them. What you are looking for is an attitude change that leads to the heart change. When they are willing to talk it through you have been successful with reset, even if they didn't initially "head to reset" in the exact location. You might finish the conversation with something like, "When I ask you to go to reset, I want you to go and trust me knowing that I will listen to your perspective. I really want us to work as a team to make our family the best that we can and that includes you following directions when you are asked to go to reset."

> **Stop and Reflect**
>
> Review the five strategies for keeping reset on track when your kids are resistant. What will be most challenging for you? How will you remind yourself "in the moment"?

Now that we understand the purpose and challenges of reset, we are better prepared to talk about the relationship between repair and consequences in the next chapter. But don't rush on too quickly. Make sure you spend the time teaching your kids the reset process. Try it for a few days and then evaluate the process together.

USING RESET EFFECTIVELY

Putting Reset Families into Practice in Five Minutes or Less

Keep doing the foundational work you have started with your family. You are in the process of building relationships that increase trust and make discipline more effective. Now you are ready to introduce the behavior self-management approach with your kids.

- Review the nonverbal cue and precision request that you decided on, and talk with your kids about how those reminders are working as gentle reminders to manage their own behavior.
- Explain the purpose of reset to your kids—emphasizing that it is not punishment.
- Explain how reset works
  - Location: decide where it will be
  - Reset expectations: how will you know they are ready to reset and move on?
  - Go through the reset sheet with the kids
  - Set up the plan should they delay or refuse; this increases buy-in.
- Now you are ready to use the three steps of redirection, including reset.

Further Resources, page 185

RESET FAMILIES

Pre-school adaptation

During the reset process the child is asked to go to the reset spot by themselves. When calm, hand them the reset sheet and take the time to go through the sheet with them

- **Questions #1 (Refer to the Sheet)**
  - It is best to tell them the behavior that sent them to reset by saying something like, "When you screamed and ran away instead of putting on your shoes, what choice were you making? Then allow the child to circle the appropriate choice.
  - When asked to remember or explain what happened if they get overwhelmed and frustrated, and don't have the words to describe what happened, take the time to reinforce and teach them. When prompted with why they were sent to reset, they can often figure out and circle the behavior choice.

- **Question #2 – What can you do next time this happens?**
  - They may have some good ideas, or you may need to give them ideas

- **Question #3 – "I need to _____ to fix it and get back to green."**
  - Read the question and allow the child time to come up with ideas of repair. They may need prompting.

- **Questions #4 – "Can you do it now?"**
  - Have them circle "yes" or "no". If they answer "no" ask them if they need help with fixing it?

When they have finished reset, and they have completed repair, which in most cases at this age is immediate, allow them to erase the laminated sheet to indicate that they are "restored" to green.

Chapter 7

Consequences as Teaching Tools

To this point in the book, we have been talking about the importance of creating a family culture that will help our kids gain the skills to become self-managers. We believe that they are strong and smart and that they can make good choices. But so often we end up reacting in a moment of frustration and go back to our default parenting style. When we take time to think about our children as self-managers, it helps us to avoid power struggles and nattering with our kids. Being a self-manager is important for our kids as they grow and mature. It is important to our family if we are going to be able to move toward our shared family vision.

We have been encouraging you to teach your kids to identify their feelings so that they can tell when they are getting close to losing control and avoid making a poor choice out of anger or frustration. "Take a break" is a strategy for them to temporarily pause a task you have asked them to complete so that they can reflect and make a positive choice. Often, this pause allows them to be the self-manager, rather than the caregiver, managing their behavior for them. If they are able to manage their behavior and return to the task you asked them to do, there is no need for any redirection. They have successfully taken control of their behavior and are well on the road to become self-managers. This is a big deal.

It is such an important life skill for your child to notice when they are not in the right space to make good decisions, and to pause before they say or do something they're going to regret. This is true in parenting, in marriage, at work, and almost any situation where frustration, anger, or grief can build. When your child demonstrates the ability to recognize the emotion building, take a break and then come back around to the task; be sure you take time to give them specific praise. In fact, look for opportunities frequently to praise the behavior you wish to see. It is so beneficial to give greater attention to the right behaviors. But the default for most of us is to take for granted the right behavior and only notice, call out, or give energy to the wrong behavior choices. You can make an intentional choice to give your energy to the best in your children, rather than the worst.

Of course, if you're going to catch them doing the right stuff, and praise them for it, you need to make sure you both know what the right stuff is. Expectations are a critical part of a kid's being able to self-manage behavior. They have to know in a concrete specific way what they are expected to do. Chapter four outlined a strategy for you to use with your family to clarify the family expectations that reflect your vision and values. Don't forget to keep coming back to this. There will be times when you realize your kids aren't clear on an expectation. Instead of getting frustrated day after day, take the time to teach or reteach the expectation in concrete terms that your kids can understand.

When the family culture is catching on, the emotional supports are in place, and the expectations are clear—your family is poised for success with the three-step strategy, called redirection. This gives your kids additional support to learn the skill of becoming a self-manager. It is easy for us as parents to get focused on changing the behavior immediately and to become discouraged when the change doesn't come fast enough. Remember, this approach to parenting focuses on helping our kids gain the skills to manage their own behavior and that takes time. But in the end, there is less nagging, fewer power struggles, more respectfulness, responsible behavior, and stronger family relationships. It is worth the investment.

One of the key components of Reset Families is consistent feedback. In this chapter we are going to take a step back and look at motivation and how our feedback works to help our kids continue

CONSEQUENCES AS TEACHING TOOLS

to make positive choices and discourages the negative behavior that is bound to surface.

Unfortunately, the word consequence has a negative connotation, but consequences themselves can be positive or negative. Let's think of the feedback we give our kids as consequences, and those consequences are results. In other words, our need to use the reminders to redirect their behavior is the consequence of their behavior choice. When your child exhibits super green behavior, your specific verbal praise (feedback) is the consequence of their outstanding behavior. In other words, the feedback (consequence) is a result of their behavior choice.

The same is true when your child makes a poor behavior choice. The feedback (reminders and reset) is the consequence of their behavior as well as a result of that choice. This is important to understand if we are going to help our child see that they are in control, rather than the victim of their parents' anger or frustration. Their behavior choice, whether positive or negative, is met with your feedback (praise, rewards, reminders, reset) and is a direct result of their behavior choice. The consequences our kids receive for their behavior determines how likely they are to repeat those behaviors. This applies to both positive and negative behaviors.

So far, we have been emphasizing the importance of giving specific positive feedback when our kids are meeting or exceeding expectations. We have talked about specific praise and how important that is to reinforcing the behavior we want to see. This type of praise is an example of a positive consequence. Hopefully you have been doing a great job of noticing what your kids are doing right.

We know that attention is a powerful reinforcer for behavior. As we learned, when we pay attention to negative behavior and engage our kids in power struggles, we often inadvertently reinforce that negative behavior of acting out to get our attention. It is equally powerful to support the behavior we want to see. That is why we spend so much time encouraging you to look for the positive rather than giving attention to the negative behaviors. If you remember from our discussion on redirection, we give reminders and then walk away without engaging, thereby ignoring the negative behavior.

With all our best efforts to notice and specifically reinforce our kids' behavior when they are meeting expectations, we know there are times that they simply are not self-managers, and we must jump in and help them learn how to better manage their behavior.

What Do We Need to Know about Consequences?

We can think about consequences as a powerful form of feedback to discourage our child's negative-behavior choice. Some people refer to these as negative consequences, but we prefer to look at consequences from a different perspective. As we mentioned earlier, consequences are simply the results of the child's behavior choice. Consequences are the feedback for our kids, as well as for us as parents, about how the child's behavior and our response is working.

In this chapter we will emphasize three attributes of effective consequences. When these attributes are applied, it can help kids recognize the connection between their behaviors and the outcomes or results they are experiencing. We can't promise your kids will like the consequences. Nor can we guarantee you'll never hear "that's not fair." But if you apply the three attributes when you are determining consequences, your child is more likely to see them as fair. We will focus on making our consequences related, reasonable, and restorative.

The loss of a privilege can be an example of a reasonable and, hopefully, related consequence. When our child chooses to engage in screen time before he has finished his homework, an expectation we agreed on together, as a parent you decide on a consequence. The loss of screen privileges for a given amount of time would be a related consequence. So the loss of his screen time makes sense with his choice to disregard the agreed-on expectation. Hopefully you have decided with them in advance what types of consequences will occur, so they are able to see that the consequence is the outcome of their choice rather than your anger.

But it's impossible to think of every behavior your child may choose. If you haven't talked about the consequence of a specific behavior in advance, the fact that the consequence is directly related to the behavior is helpful in guiding your kids to connect their consequence to their choice. They are empowered. They are more likely to see that they can make choices that lead to a different reality.

Effective consequences are not punitive or used out of frustration. The most important thing about consequences is that we do not exhibit a punitive attitude when our child's behavior frustrates us. This is such an easy trap to fall into. Our child is being defiant or disrespectful, so we respond by heaping consequence upon consequence. Or our child is being oppositional, so we think of the one thing they want to do most this week and take it away, out of anger, sending them into a tailspin.

Consequences given in the heat of the moment or out of frustration rarely have the impact we hope they will. Instead of causing our child to reflect on their behavior choices and take responsibility for their reality, we tick our kids off. They lose sight of their choices and instead focus on how mean or controlling we are as parents. That is why using the reminders, followed by reset, is such an asset. It gives time for both the parent and the child to settle down and make better choices.

Again, we are not suggesting kids will like the consequences, but we do believe they can get to the point where they see the connection between their behavior choices and the consequences they are experiencing. We will give you some tools to help you make consequences effective even when they feel negative to your child.

Parents often get nervous when the topic of consequences comes up because they think they have to come up with the right response to stop their child's behavior immediately. That makes it feel much more like a life-and-death situation than it really is. It is more a matter of trial and error than of life and death. So let's dive in and figure out some ways that we can be more effective in figuring out the right consequences. In order to do that we need to think back to our discussion on reset to make sure we connect consequences correctly to reset.

Reset and Consequences

Initially having to go to reset is designed to stop a negative behavior, not to change it. When the child is sent to reset, we want to communicate that the behavior must stop. That is why some kids may see reset as a negative consequence. Being sent to reset stops the behavior, but the change happens during the restorative part of reset. That is the teaching time where you appeal to their heart and the values you have established as a family.

It is important to help the kids understand that what they see as negative consequences are the result of them failing to manage their own behavior. Remember, your child is not a victim, and you are not the bad guy. Eventually they will see that they have a choice. It is much easier for them to learn the lesson if you do not use anger and frustrated tone of voice or body language.

Change happens during the restorative part of reset as they change their attitude and behavior. Sometimes the process of reset is enough of a consequence to help a child get behavior back on track. The undesired behavior has been stopped by the use of reset. The child owns the mistake and is ready to make that right choice instead. No major relational damage has been done. It was a minor offense. In that case, you don't need a long, drawn-out process or unnecessary repairs or consequences. Your reset process only needs to include a brief but clear description of the desired behavior.

Once they get it and are willing to take the opportunity to make a positive behavior choice, you are done. You can completely undo the lesson if you repeat yourself or get into a lecture about it. Reset and move on. The change in their attitude and behavior is the evidence of restoration. It's always great to provide positive reinforcement when your child is able to accept responsibility in reset. You may say something like, "I knew you could do it!"

CONSEQUENCES AS TEACHING TOOLS

> **Stop and Reflect**
>
> Quickly identify a time that you saw your child "get it" and change their behavior after they had owned their problem and faced the consequences. How would you describe their attitude? If you are having trouble remembering a time, think about the evidence you might see in the child when they get it. What are we looking for?

Now that we understand the importance of using consequences as teaching tools, rather than resorting to punitive measures to make our kids suffer for their poor choices, let's talk about ways we can make sure we are coming up with consequences that are effective.

Three *R*s of Consequences

When considering a consequence, it's important to ask ourselves if it is related, reasonable, and restorative.

Related Consequences

Let's begin with what we mean by related. Effective consequences are *related* to the behavior. Consequences should be natural or logical whenever possible. That means that they should have something to do with the behavior that led to the consequence and should help the child learn from his mistake. To benefit from a natural consequence, a child needs to be able to apply what they've learned to their future behaviors.

Natural consequences do not work well on younger children. Really young children lack the ability to understand that the consequence is a direct result of their behavior. They don't understand cause and effect. For example, if you let a four-year-old choose his own bedtime, he won't likely relate feeling tired and acting out the next day to staying up late. It is unlikely this natural consequence will cause the child to decide to go to bed earlier in the future. However, a teenager who stays on their video games too long and is late for work should have the ability to connect their behavior choice to the trouble they got into from their boss. The key word here is *should*.

Some of our cultural practices may not help our kids own their behavior choices or take responsibility for their contribution to a situation. It's tempting to blame others, or in this case, to think of the boss as a jerk, rather than take responsibility for the behavior that led to the situation in the first place.

That is why Reset Families is a practical parenting approaching. Learning to accept responsibility for the consequences of our behavior choices is the only way to learn for those choices, move on, and make better choices in the future. When they are related, it is easier for our kids to make the connection.

Consequences that are related teach problem-solving, healthy decision-making skills, and help parents avoid power struggles. They help kids understand ways they can make better decisions in the future and remind the child that they are in control, not the victim of your anger. Natural and related consequences are teaching them to pause and think about the implications of their behavior choice when the consequences are still small. Before long they will be making decisions that have much larger life implications. Learning the cause and effect of natural consequences is valuable in the short term but is also an important life skill.

When kids are spared any consequences, they are more likely to focus on their parents' unwillingness to allow them to do something rather than taking responsibility for their behavior. For example, a teenager may focus on thinking his mother is mean for not allowing him to stay up late, rather than focusing on the fact that if he doesn't take responsibility for getting the proper amount of sleep, he'll have difficulty getting up for school on time.

Related consequences help children connect their behavior choice to the real world. Remind them that their behavior is a choice! Appropriate consequences help children start to think about relating possible consequences of their actions to a particular behavior as they begin to make decisions for themselves. For example, because they didn't finish the chores, they won't be able to go with a friend who just stopped by to invite them to go bowling.

As a parent, it is often tempting to rescue our kids from the natural consequences of their behavior choices. Natural consequences can teach, *but* only if no one interferes. If your child forgot their cleats at home, they miss out on practice. They probably won't do it again. If they forgot their lunch, they may be hungry or have to charge a hot lunch and pay for it themselves. If they spent all their money on junk food instead of choosing to save, they might not be able to buy that game they really want when it goes on sale.

But in each of these situations, great parents with big hearts and the best of intentions often rescue their children. I know, because these are real-life examples from my house. Instead of my kids missing practice, they have called me, and I have run home, got their cleats, dropped them at school, and raced back to work. Or instead of them missing out on that great sale, I have offered the child a loan that they can work off or pay back when they get their allowance. Each time we rescue our child from one of these natural consequences, we are depriving them of the opportunity to learn how their behavior choices affect their reality. It is much easier to learn these lessons when it costs you a day of practice than it is to learn after it has cost you your job.

Effective consequences are usually immediate and of short duration, making them easier to track and enforce. The more immediate time frame helps the child see how the consequence is a natural outcome of their behavior choice. It also prevents you from forgetting the episode and missing the opportunity for the lesson the child needs. I can't tell you how many times my poor parents forgot who was grounded, who didn't have screens, or who owed their allowance for a debt. With four kids, or even with one, it's hard to remember. That's why immediate consequences are such a great solution. They provide immediate feedback, and there is nothing for the parent to remember.

As we have emphasized before, immediate consequences make it easier for any child to connect the behavior with the consequence. Developmentally, this is especially important when children are younger; the consequence must come immediately if they are to understand the connection with the behavior. This helps to ensure that kids remember why they received the consequence in the first place. If it's delayed by a week, they're more likely to forget. Taking away your child's overnight with Grandma that is planned for next week is not likely to be as effective as having them do extra chores today.

There are a couple of exceptions to the situation of immediate consequences. When your children are older, it's okay to have them lose something over the weekend, such as losing technology because of a major loss of trust issue, or missing out on a planned activity with friends. Also, practically speaking, sometimes delayed consequences are necessary. You may need time to cool down. In that situation, it is not only okay but wise to delay consequences. The important thing is, you can't forget. You need to come back around and enforce consequences. You may say something like "We will discuss this later. I need time to think about appropriate repair." Ideally you will follow through before the day is out.

In addition, sometimes it's not possible to give immediate consequences. If you find out your child got into trouble on the bus three days ago, the consequence will have obviously been delayed, because you didn't know about it immediately. Or if she misbehaves right before she gets on the bus in the morning, you may need to wait until she gets home from school before you can give her a consequence. The sense of immediacy is based on when you found out about the infraction. Immediate starts then! By taking the time to stop and think before you hand out the consequence will help ensure that the consequence is related to the behavior.

Effective Consequences Are Reasonable

Do your best to keep emotions out of your consequences. Take the time you need to calm down before setting consequences. If you feel like grounding them for a month, you might not be ready to discuss consequences. Reset gives both you and your child time to think. Avoid spouting something out of anger that you simply can't

CONSEQUENCES AS TEACHING TOOLS

enforce. For example, "you have to stay home the rest of the day" when you have an appointment later, and they have to go with you. Be careful about being unreasonable.

Be sure you are able to follow through with your consequence and that it's reasonable to do so. Remember, your ability to stay calm, and teach through consequences, will affect whether your child sees that the consequence resulted from their choice, rather than turning their attention to your unreasonable behavior. It is also less likely that they will feel like a victim of your anger.

As the saying goes, "Little dings for little things." Small consequences are adequate for minor infractions of the expectations. Lower your tolerance level for behavior infractions. Don't just grit your teeth and hope the behavior will change. Respond before you are angry so the behavior and consequence remain small. Remember, you must respond or the behavior will continue to escalate. So act quickly to give them a chance to repair their behavior. If you engage the system while the behaviors are small, you can often avoid the behavior growing into something more difficult to repair.

Knowing the child's currency will help you keep them reasonable. What is a reasonable consequence for one of your children may not be for the other. Kids have different personalities and value different things. It is good to create a list of consequences that would work for each of your kids. Involve your child by asking them what they believe the consequences should be before problem behaviors arise. That will let you know what is important to them. You can use their suggestions when they fail to meet expectations making it more difficult for the child to argue. If you can't get them to be reasonable about consequences for their own behavior, consider taking another tack and asking what the consequence should be if a sibling engages in a specific behavior.

Consequences don't have to last a long time. I know, this is hard to swallow, but it's true. Most of us grew up in the age of grounding. Much like a jail sentence, "You do the crime, you do the time." It didn't really matter what the offense was, they pretty much all earned the same penalty—"You're grounded." The only variable was how long you would be grounded, and maybe what exactly you were grounded from. It's hard to imagine that a consequence that can be done and over within a matter of minutes or maybe hours could be effective. But if it's related and it's reasonable, that consequence can have just as much—or even more—impact on a child's future behavior choices than consequences that last a week.

Not only do consequences not have to last a long time, they also should be used sparingly. Now, perhaps some of you are thinking, *You don't know my child. I'd love to use consequences sparingly, but it's one thing after another with that child.* In that case, you may have to figure out what behaviors will result in consequences for a while and take a different approach with the rest.

Consequences become less effective when they are used too much. Kids who lose all their privileges for an extended period of time begin to lose motivation to earn them back. They can begin to feel hopeless, internalizing the behavior and determining they are just a bad kid, and it's always going to be that way. I know it's frustrating, because as adults we're thinking, *Just stop behaving that way and it will get better,* but sometimes that's just too hard.

If you find the consequences piling up, consider going back to the drawing board with your child and extend some intentional grace. Include them in the conversation about making sure the consequences are reasonable, and recognize how they have been working hard to make change. This will reassure them that their voice will be heard and that you are willing to listen and make changes where it is appropriate.

Maybe you clean the slate or cut the consequences in half to make it more attainable for your struggling child. Don't just forget about it. Have an intentional conversation, so your child is clear on the consequences they have coming, but also your decision to let them off the hook for some things because you want them to see the way to get back to green. Remember to make the consequences manageable for you, and show respect to your child's attitude. It is better to recognize and reward any attempt they have made to meet the expectation rather than to wait until their response is perfect!

It is also important to let the child know how long the consequence will be in effect. That helps them to know when repair is completed. Saying, "You're grounded until I say so," just isn't a good motivator. Neither is saying, "You can't go anywhere until I can trust you again." The length of the consequence is somewhat related to the age of your child. A very young child needs the consequence to be immediate and done. It is not possible for them to think about their behavior choice for hours and then be expected to remember why that happened.

Usually, twenty-four hours is a good amount of time to take something away from a child. However, there may be times when the behavior infraction is so serious that you take away a privilege until your child earns it back. If this is the case, outline exactly what needs to happen for your child to earn it back. Instead of saying, "You can't have your cell phone back until I can trust you," say something like, "You can begin earning the right to use your phone for one hour a night if you get all your homework done and tell the truth about the work that is due, for the next two weeks."

Effective Consequences Are Restorative

The definition of restoration includes the idea of returning something to its former condition. That is exactly the goal of the very best types of consequences. Encouraging our kids or empowering them to return something to the way it was before it was broken. Restorative consequences are not punitive. There is a thread of vengeance implied in punishment. It contains the implication that "You need to pay for what you did." Conversely, restorative consequences imply, "You not only can, but you need to fix what you broke." That's a powerful life lesson.

It is exciting to see our kids learn how to own their mistakes, make repairs, and then move forward. Rather than carrying with them shame and self-condemnation, they are empowered to restore things to their original beauty, whether it's a space that needs cleaning or a relationship that needs healing. Rather than blaming others for their mistakes or feeling themselves a victim of outside forces, they are empowered to find what was broken through their behavior choices, restore it, and move forward. What we really want is for them is to learn to manage their behavior in a different way as a result of their reflection and consequences. We want attitude change, and that happens best when we take a restorative approach, helping them gain the skills they need to learn to manage their behavior.

Consequences should be used as a teaching tool and shouldn't shame or embarrass kids. If our actions shame and embarrass our kids, they will learn that we don't respect them and that they can't trust us to treat them in a restorative way. The best-case scenario is when the consequence leads to restoration. The child learns from his mistake and knows that it is not going to hang over his head. This is important practice for real life.

By teaching our kids accountability through reset and restoration, they are learning the skills they need to repair the damage done and move on. Another word for *repair* is *accountability*. During reset, the child learns to ask, "What damage was done (physical, emotional, spiritual or relational)?" and "What do I need to do to fix it?" Repair is essential for restoration. After discussing damage, you and the child can determine the repairs (clean up the mess, write ten other things you could do when you are angry, do chores to earn money to fix what you broke, do a service project for the sibling you offended, etc.). In the end they have learned that they can make a mistake, be accountable by owning the behavior, clean up the mess, and move on. That is true restoration!

Restoration is hopeful. It implies that with some effort, things can be made right again. Restoration leaves room for teamwork or may even require it. Because the ultimate goal is to make things right again, not to make them suffer, we can partner with our kids when necessary in the restoration process. The opportunity for teamwork lets our kids know that they are not in this alone. We can't always fix a mess we made by ourselves. Kids sometimes destroy something they can't repair. They may break something that is too hard for them to fix themselves, or they may ruin a special family activity.

In these cases, we offer them the opportunity to "restore" or "make up" by giving the time back to the person who fixes the damage. For example, if Dad has to spend Saturday morning fixing a door, then the child who broke the door may need to spend Saturday doing some of Dad's other chores. If we had to cut a playtime short at the park because of one child's behavior, maybe the siblings who weren't acting out get to choose the next family activities or TV shows for a specified period of time.

When teamwork is part of restoration, you are giving your children skills they need for the rest of their lives as you build trust and relationship. As adults, they may need help to fix a mistake made at work. Wouldn't it be great if they have already learned how to ask for help when they mess up? Other times, they may need the help of a counselor to help them work through a mind-set or belief system that is holding them back. If they know that restoration sometimes takes teamwork, they may be willing to ask for help when the problem is smaller, rather than wait until it has wreaked havoc in their lives.

> **Stop and Reflect**
>
> So now that we've reviewed the three R's of consequences (Related, Reasonable, and Restorative), we want to encourage you to take a moment to practice applying those principles to real situation families face. On page 185, in "Further References," you will find Come Up with Some Natural Consequences Sheet, a list of yellow behavior choices (choices that fail to meet our expectation) for each behavior choice. Try to think of a consequence that meets the three R's criteria.
>
> Now think of a consequence for one of your child's challenging behaviors:
>
> - Think of a challenging behavior you face with one of your children.
> - Think about consequences that meet the specifications of the three *R*s

You can see that it is not always easy to come up with the appropriate consequence. This will get easier as you begin to apply consequences, not as punishment, but as a teaching tool when your child displays a particularly challenging behavior. If you make consequences related, reasonable, and restorative you will teach your kids the skills they need to navigate life as you continue building strong family relationships. The three *R*s are your guideline to evaluate the effectiveness of your consequences. When consequences don't seem to be working well, take the time to make sure they are meeting the Related, Reasonable, and Restorative criteria.

Making Consequences Effective

We have been talking about building strong family relationships and working to balance those relationships with self-management and accountability. When you have a strong relationship but hesitate to hold your child accountable for their behavior, the two are out of balance. You destroy the relationship that you have worked so hard to build when you don't provide the security and boundaries that come when they know you will follow through. On the other hand, if you are applying expectations in an unfair manner, or are inconsistent, you end up with the same result and damage trusted relationships.

If you throw relationship out the window by trying to get compliance at all costs, you are sacrificing relationship. When your kids are grown, they are left with the lessons they learned through accountability growing up, and the relationship you have built over time. When you are able to keep accountability and relationship in balance, you will build strong family connections that are able to move you toward your shared family vision and through all the seasons of life yet to come.

Be Consistent with Your Consequences

If you make consequences related, reasonable, and restorative, *consistency* is the secret to making them effective. That helps your kids know what to expect and that you will follow through.

Enforce the consequences no matter how much your children whine, beg, or promise to change their behavior. Once they can see how they are related to the expectations and a respectful family rela-

CONSEQUENCES AS TEACHING TOOLS

tionship, they need to experience the natural consequences in order to learn. You can recognize and praise their willingness to try, but you must enforce the consequence so they will know you mean what you say.

For example, if you take away your child's video games only two out of every three times that he refuses to get off when his time is up, he'll quickly learn he's got a good chance of getting away with staying on his game system. He will believe it's worth the risk. Another example: if you tell your child he can't go out and play for the rest of the day, but by afternoon you change your mind and let him go outside anyway, he won't learn. If, however, you are consistent in giving him a consequence each and every time, his behavior will change.

Like we said before, this does not mean there is never room for grace. Grace can be a powerful and effective teaching tool too. But it has to be intentional. It cannot appear that you have gotten distracted or changed your mind about the consequence. If you are changing your mind because you were unreasonable, admit your mistake to your child and adjust the consequence. If you are changing your mind, because they have shown a clear change in attitude and you wish to be gracious, let them know how they have demonstrated accountability and why you are adjusting the consequence. Sometimes, rather than changing the consequence, you can stick to the original consequence, but try to make it a little less miserable by making yourself available to play a game or do a fun activity for a while. Then you have shown compassion and demonstrated consistency to the consequence. If they whine or beg it's not wise to give in, not even once. It will teach them that begging or pestering works, and they will try that approach on every consequence in the future.

Challenges with Consequences

Now let's go over a couple of common challenges with consequences:

If your child says "I don't care" when you give them the consequence, tune it out. Many times, their response "I don't care" is an attempt to draw you into an argument, to try and save face or to try and get out of the consequences they have earned. It is important to tune it out or respond by saying something like "I understand that you don't care, but those are the consequences." Then stick with them. Don't get pulled into a power struggle or be tempted to heap consequences on because of their attitude. Allow your consistency to speak for itself.

If your child uses attention-seeking behaviors such as whining, temper tantrums, or asking the same question repeatedly, actively ignore those behaviors. Actively ignoring their behavior is part of the redirection system we have been learning. We say "actively ignoring" because this is hard work. It is not easy to ignore a child who is throwing a tantrum. But this is how you avoid being drawn into a power struggle. Your response will vary by the age of your child, but ignoring is especially effective with young children.

During the reset time, if you are going to ignore whining, it might be good to let them know that you will ignore them and walk away when they whine or scream so they understand that you are ignoring their behavior, not them. With young kids you may need to remind them about whining at first by saying something like "I can't hear you when you whine." Then walk away. Their negative behavior will escalate at first, because they are not getting the response they want—your attention. But as soon as the behavior stops, go right to the child and say something like "Sammy, great job sitting there quietly. Now let's talk about what we can do instead of going to Grandma's house since she is sick." This will reinforce your child for being calm, rather than for using whining or screaming.

If your parental instinct says ignoring is not the right response to this particular emotional response, then speak to the emotion underneath the behavior, rather than the behavior itself. Sometimes kids will "ping" because they are looking for reassurance rather than acting out of defiance. It feels a great deal like whining, but it is important to try and get at the underlying emotion that is the source of that behavior. There is nothing wrong with responding to the need they are expressing, even if they are expressing it in the wrong way. For example, a child who is constantly seeking our attention may be reassured not by our answering their incessant questions, but rather by addressing the need behind the question. Instead of answering their questions, they may just need to know you see them, you're still there, you care about them. Instead of saying "Stop yelling," you might say "It looks like you are really overwhelmed, can I help you?" If the child is open to emotional support, feel free to give it. If they are stuck in their tantrum behavior, go back to actively ignoring.

Part of the balance we are always trying to achieve between accountability and relationship is looking for clues to the behavior. It is not easy to use consequences as teaching tools. For most of us, our defaults are set somewhere closer to the ends of the spectrum: rules and compliance first, and then relationship *or* relationship at all cost, with little to no accountability. Somewhere between these ends of the spectrum is a middle ground where consequences are used as teaching tools and relationships can be strengthened even in the midst of correction. We consistently use consequences as teaching tools because we love our children and want what's best for them. Whether you're tempted to be authoritarian or tempted to be permissive, choose the balanced approach because that's the approach that provides solid footing for your child's future.

Putting Reset Families into Practice in Five Minutes or Less

- Check in with your kids to evaluate how they are doing at meeting expectations. See how they feel about the way the system is working.
- Clarify the consequence for failing to go to reset or specify one if you have not done so.
- Think about one or two expectations that need work in your family. Review them with the kids and ask them what they think an appropriate consequence would be if they chose not to respond to redirection.
- Take this opportunity to explain that it is not punishment you are after, but that you want to help them find things that will motivate them to manage their own behavior. The consequence is a result of their failure not to manage their behavior.

Hopefully, each week, you are intentionally setting aside a time to spend with the family to have fun but also to have some of the discussions that will help support them with the new system that you are implementing.

Further Resources, Page 185

CHAPTER 8

Rewards that Build Relationships

We have emphasized throughout the entire book that the attention we give our kids is a powerful reinforcer to support the behavior we want to see. Sometimes our attention may inadvertently reward negative behavior when we give it at the wrong time and in the wrong way. It is important to respond to behavior that is not meeting expectations with the three reminders, waiting to engage in the final step until the child is ready to complete the reset process. That gives the child time to deescalate so that they can process rationally.

We have also talked a great deal about creating a family culture that encourages and supports the child with the skills necessary to manage their own behavior. One of the first skills we introduced was "take a break," where we watch for triggers that begin to escalate a child to the point that they are overwhelmed or frustrated. At that point, we encourage the child to take a moment to calm down and think about what they could do to solve their problem and manage their behavior in a positive way, rather than lashing out in anger or frustration. Sometimes that involves asking the child questions to help them identify their feelings and strategize a solution together. But hopefully the child will eventually choose to use that tool on their own, creating the space they need to think creatively about solutions.

In the last chapter, we talked about balancing our family relationships by encouraging self-management as well as asking for accountability through the use of consequences. When we apply expectations consistently and enforce them fairly, we avoid doing damage to the trusted relationships we have built. We talked about the importance of consequences that let our children experience the natural results of their behavior choices. It is important that the consequences we use are related to the behavior that was off target, that they are reasonable and as immediate as possible. We also suggested that consequences should always be restorative, aimed at restoring what was lost. Whether it is a relationship, or something in the physical world, restorative consequences lead to personal learning that will strengthen relationships.

Nothing jeopardizes restoration as much as a hint of punishment. It is easy to resort to a default style of parenting when we are deciding consequences. Like we said in the last chapter, it often feels like they need to "pay for what they did." However, that works against the notion of restoration, because it suggests punishment, which contains that thread of vengeance. Rather than a focus on punishment, we want to use consequences that teach our child the skills they need so that they can own their behavior choice, come up with a plan for next time, make the repairs necessary to maintain relationship, and move on.

Even though we give consequences out of love, they are still no fun. So we want to turn the page to focus on something that is more fun. In this chapter, we will explore how we can make consequences most effective by implementing them with rewards. Before we get too far into discussing rewards, it is important to discuss the difference between bribes and rewards. How often have you witnessed a parent at the cash register trying to check out and pay for the groceries with a child writhing around on the floor begging for what seems to be the strategically placed candy? In a moment of embarrassment and with an intense desire to put an end to the scene, the parent says, "Get up off the floor and quit screaming and I will give you the candy." So what just happened? They solved the problem, right? Both the parent and the child got what they wanted. However, most of us would feel this was not exactly a win-win for the long run.

REWARDS THAT BUILD

Bribes and Rewards – What Is the Difference?

In order to determine the difference between a bride and reward, let's take a look at the definition of a bribe. According to the Cambridge Dictionary,[11] a bribe is, *"The act of giving someone money or something else of value . . . to persuade that person to do something you want."* In the case of parenting, once the relief of the immediate solution wears off, the realization of the price we have paid may cause us pause.

In contrast, a reward is defined in the Oxford Dictionary[12] as *"Something given in recognition of one's service, effort, or achievement."* With both bribes and rewards the child is getting something for doing what you want him to do and you have resolved your immediate and frustrating challenge. However, using rewards rather than bribes helps you build a trusted working relationship with your child rather than being manipulated. Let's take a deeper look at bribes first, since they are usually very effective in the moment and they are often a first instinct in a challenging and potentially embarrassing situation.

So Just What Are Bribes?

When thinking back to the grocery-store scene, bribes are used to get the desired behavior by setting a price or desired outcome and usually to get the outcome quickly. Not only that, generally, bribery generally occurs under duress right smack in the middle of a situation where all you want is to change your child's behavior on the spot. In the pressure of the very uncomfortable moment, you offer him something that you had no previous intention of offering.

Bribery usually occurs when both you and your child are overwhelmed and frustrated, and it may become a form of negotiation that puts the child in the driver's seat. It can lead to an attitude of entitlement; they won't "work" without the "pay" they have learned to expect in advance. Bribery can become an ongoing pattern that ultimately teaches your child to act out to get what he wants. Kids can come to expect something extra for simply executing their daily responsibilities. For example, John doesn't want to clean his room.

He's sitting on the floor with his arms crossed and says he's not going to do it. Mom enters and says, "Johnny, if you clean your room you can have some ice cream." Mom has just set a price for Johnny to clean his room. This time, it's a bowl of ice cream. That's a bribe. Because Johnny is pouting, mom offers him something she had no previous intention of offering.

That's how bribes work. In fear that you won't get what you want any other way, you agree to "pay" to get what you want. How is that different from offering a reward? The effective use of rewards is quite different from bribery because you are compensating your child for her choice to follow expectations, usually after the fact, rather than being manipulated in the moment. Bribes say, "If you . . . I will give you . . ." Rewards say, "Because you did . . . you get . . ."

Rewards are something given in recognition of service, effort, or achievement on the part of your child. In order to be most effective, they are discussed, planned for, and mutually agreed on in advance. This means that you have talked with your child ahead of time and have set goals together. The discussion of goals that are worth working for is the first step. The second step is considering what type of motivation in the form of a reward could be paired with that goal to make it more likely that the child will keep on the path toward the goal. A reward is a promise of what is to come as a result of the child's commitment to the goal.

Let's think back to the example of John refusing to clean his room and his mom's bribe to comply. There is a simple way to change that scene from a bribe to a reward. It requires that you offer the reward after compliance has occurred rather than before. Here's what that might look like: Mom asks Johnny to clean his room, and he sort of fusses and he stomps off to his room. Mom goes about her business, and after some time passes she notices that Johnny is back in the living room watching TV. A bit surprised, Mom says, "Johnny, I thought I asked you to clean your room." Johnny responds, "It's done."

Mom checks and sure enough, Johnny has cleaned his room. Then Mom may say something like, "Johnny, thanks so much for cleaning your room, even though you didn't want to. How about we

REWARDS THAT BUILD

sit down and have a cup of hot chocolate together!" Rather than a bribe influencing him to make the right choice, the mom changed her strategy into a reward. She ignored the storming out temporarily to reward the behavior that her son chose. So in this case, she was able to look beyond the frustration, wait for the change without engaging, and then choose to focus on his positive choice. Should Johnny remain resistant and fail to clean his room, it is important to stick with consequences rather than resorting to the bribe. When they finally comply, that is the time for the reward.

The differences may seem small, but they make all the difference in the world. A child who is bribed is likely to take an attitude of escalation until a bribe is on the table. "Why clean my room the first time I am asked? If I hold out, my parent will become desperate and bribe me to do it!" In the first scenario, if the child does what he is asked, he gets nothing for cleaning his room, except maybe a thank you. But in the second scenario, if he resists being responsible, he will end up getting something out of cleaning his room. Clearly the bribe has reinforced the wrong behavior.

So in order to qualify as a reward, the positive reinforcement is given after the behavior you requested has occurred. In the more ideal world, goals are set ahead of time, and children earn tokens or marks on a chart that they cash in for the incentive or reward that had been identified previously. Sometimes it is worth taking the time to celebrate an attempt to meet the goal, even though they failed to fully meet it. It won't be with the full reward, but if the child made a huge effort that is worth noticing and celebrating. Remember, the definition of a reward is something given in recognition of effort *or* achievement. Hard work and stick-to-itiveness is worth celebrating and the use of rewards take intentional planning and balance.

How Rewards Work

To understand how rewards work, it can be helpful to think in terms of how the work world operates. Employees do their jobs and complete the tasks required of their position, and a paycheck is the tangible reward for work accomplished. While there are numerous other ways in which work can be satisfying, the paycheck is the tangible reward. As parents, we often hope that our child will be internally motivated to meet expectations just because it is important to them. That works more effectively during some phases of development than others, but for the most part, children tend to be externally motivated first by things they want or enjoy. And honestly, let's face it: as adults, if we have a new skill to learn or a bad habit to break, we often motivate ourselves with the promise of a reward. It may be in the form of an external reward given by the boss after we have completed training, or a reward we designate such as guilt-free movie watching after we have reached our goal.

Rewards are very powerful tools you can use with your child. However, they are easy to misuse in the hopes of encouraging our kid to come around and "want" to do the right thing. As we mentioned earlier, it is fine to celebrate a valiant effort with some form of reward, even when they didn't completely make their goal. However, the original reward promised must be withheld until they meet the goal completely. I know this is hard for some of you. It is for me. I love to give good things to my kids. But if children are given rewards regardless of behavior for whatever reason, we have inadvertently rewarded negative or at the very least, possibly passive behavior. As a result, the incentive to practice new skills and put in the effort required to reach goals will be undermined or will disappear altogether.

Making Rewards Effective

The important thing to keep in mind here is that the success of rewards begins and ends with relationship. You have been working hard to build strong family connections. That prepares the way for you to work with your kids to set behavioral goals that are worth working toward. As you set those behavioral goals you have the opportunity to motivate them by establishing an appropriate reward they will receive when they have achieved that specific and concrete goal.

One of the main objectives of rewards is to encourage your kids to keep working toward worthwhile goals. Along the way it will be

REWARDS THAT BUILD

important that you give them positive intervention with the redirection system if they begin to get off track and begin to move away from the goal. We are in the business of helping our kids gain the skills to manage their own behavior, and that takes time and our commitment to teaching them the skills they need, rather than reacting to their momentary failure with anger and frustration. On the other hand, you have the opportunity to be their number one cheerleader offering positive support as you recognize evidence of their progress toward the behavioral goal you have chosen together.

Since you have continued this far into this book you are demonstrating your interest in becoming the best caregiver you can be. If you have been practicing the skills outlined in the previous chapters, you are ready to learn how to put the bow on the package. In the parenting journey, we are in it for the long haul. Though there are times it seems like our kids have grown overnight, at other times it seems like the change we want will never happen.

Real change, the physical, emotional, and behavioral change we are looking for, develops over time. As parents we need to be able to spot even small places of progress. It may be easy for some to look back and think, not enough or not good enough. That response only sows seeds of frustration and hopelessness in our child. But during the times when change seems slow, remember to celebrate the positive even if it appears to be a long way from your goal. Hopefully you are seeing change in your family relationships and now it is time to think about how you can encourage and support the growth that you see.

It is important that you work to make the rewards you offer increasingly effective in building strong relationships with your child as well as reinforcing the behavioral skills they are learning. Here are some suggestions that will help rewards be more effective for your family.

1. Understand Your Child's Currency

First, in order to make your rewards more effective, it is helpful to take the time to try and understand your child's currency. We briefly mentioned this in the last chapter. Every person is different and therefore it makes sense that what motivates each person will be different too. We are not trying to discover what our children value most so that we can manipulate them. Our willingness to offer rewards that have value to them demonstrates that we want to support them in making progress toward goals.

Depending on your child's wiring, personality, areas of interest, and age you will need to figure out what they find motivating and then adapt your approach with them. This communicates that you value them enough to find ways to adapt the "system" to fit them individually.

Another factor to keep in is that when it comes to rewards, one size does not fit all. One of the best things we can do is take the time to really get to know our child, in all their uniqueness and then "speak their language" when we are attempting to motivate or reward them.

In addition, your kids have hobbies, interests, favorites, and all kinds of preferences that you can use to personalize their rewards. Once again, the goal in recognizing this currency is to communicate value and respect rather than to create a list of ways to manipulate your child. That's what we mean when we say effective discipline is all about relationship. It matters in each area of our lives, but especially if we want to authentically reward our kids.

Another great way to understand your child's currency is to learn how your kids express and receive love. In *The Five Love Languages of Children*, authors Gary Chapman and Ross Campbell[13] expand the idea of rewards to include more than tangible things. When we understand our kid's way of expressing and receiving love, two things will happen. Not only will we be able to reward them in ways that matter to them, we'll also be able to express love to them in ways that actually make them feel loved and valued. The five love languages mentioned in the book are Physical Touch, Words of Affirmation, Quality Time, Gifts, and Acts of Service. To get an idea of your child's love language you can always check out 5lovelanguages.com and have your children take the survey especially designed for kids. You can even help them determine your own love language.

To give you a head start thinking about love languages, here are some attributes Chapman and Campbell suggest for kids with each love language:

Physical Touch: This child loves kisses and hugs. They may like to wrestle, sit in your lap, cuddle, or be close. They seek out your physical affection.

Words of Affirmation: These kids light up at a compliment. They remember the nice things you say about them long after you have forgotten. Conversely the criticism you offer packs quite a punch. They probably keep notes you have written. Whether it's public or private they thrive on your specific praise.

Quality Time: This child wants time set aside to spend with you. It doesn't have to be elaborate, but it does have to be intentional and frequent. When you go through busy seasons and aren't connect with this child, it will show.

Gifts: Sometimes we think it's not ok to want gifts as a sign of love, but some kids love this tangible expression. The gifts don't have to be elaborate. It may be their favorite treat brought home from the store or a beautiful leaf because they told you how excited they were for fall. It could be anything in their favorite color.

Acts of Service: This love language is a hard one to detect in kids because we do so many things to serve them. But, kids with this love language are going to be very grateful when you serve them in some way. Taking care of something they can do themselves is a way of expressing love.

2. Praising Great Choices

You can also make rewards more effective in motivating behavior change by praising great choices frequently. As you give praise, be sure to tie it back to the desired behavior. For example, we would say, "Thank you for being so responsible and starting your homework without even being asked."

This takes us back to our discussion about noticing the behaviors we want to see. We have encouraged you to notice both green behavior—behavior that meets your family expectations and super green behaviors, those that go above and beyond what you expect. When you notice good or great behavior choices use specific, concrete, and authentic praise, along with a genuine pat on the back when your child makes progress toward a goal that is challenging for them. Use words like, "I knew you could do it! I am so proud of you."

When offering praise, remember that praising the effort that went into something, rather than simply the achievement itself, helps develop a growth mind-set. In *Mindset: The New Psychology of Success*,[14] Carol Dweck suggests that kids who are told that they are smart when they do well on a test tend to fear failure. They become anxious about maintaining the perception that they are smart and may avoid taking risks, thereby developing a fixed mind-set. They believe they are smart until they have experiences that demonstrate the opposite.

On the other hand, kids who do well, but are praised for the effort they must have put into doing well, develop a growth mind-set. They believe that if they suffer a setback, they can make adjustments and succeed again in the future. This is a great principle to keep in mind when you are praising your children. Praise the work, effort, growth you see in them, not just the fixed attributes. When your daughter comes home with an A on her math test, instead of simply saying, "Wow, you're really smart," you would instead say, "I love how hard you worked on your homework so you could do your best on this test." Or if your son wins the big game, instead of saying, you are so strong or fast, you might say, "I love the way you practice hard every day so you can be successful at the game."

Be generous with your praise. Many people worry about spoiling their children or inflating their ego. It may be true that if you praise your child every single time they do anything right, even things that are simple for them, they are more likely to develop an overinflated ego. However, they are more likely to think you're insincere. When praise is spontaneous and sincere, you don't need to worry about adverse side effects like inflated egos.

Most of us don't struggle with noticing too much of the good our kids do. In fact, it's quite the opposite. In the busyness of life, we often fail to notice the good at all, instead focusing our thoughts and our attention on what needs to change. Noticing more of what our kids are getting right and appreciating the effort, even with verbal praise, can not only strengthen your connection but can also be a strong motivator for positive behavior choices.

Verbal praise is powerful. Rewarding your child for something they did that was meeting or exceeding expectations is a great way to encourage them to make those choices in the future even when you are not watching. These rewards can be "on the spot." No system is needed. Simply be on the lookout for great choices, tie them back to the family expectation and reward the child with whatever makes sense in the moment. Remember, it doesn't have to happen every time but frequently enough that they see you are noticing their effort, not just when they are not meeting expectations.

The result is that kids know what they did specifically that was above and beyond and they feel great about doing the right thing. Sometimes it is hard to come up with words that sound authentic. As you take the time to try this out, you will land on things that work in your family. Here is an example of something you might say, "I watched you help your friend get up after he fell and you asked his friends to quit making fun of him. Thank you for being trustworthy and respectful. I know that isn't easy."

> **Stop and Reflect:**
>
> Think of one area that your child has had difficulty meeting expectations. Make a concerted effort to notice when she is meeting or exceeding the expectation and make the effort to specifically praise her. Think about an appropriate small reward you could give her the first time she is successful.

3. **Add Concrete Rewards that Reflect Your Child's Currency**

Finally, take the time to make your child's "love language" and preferences practical. *By now you* have done a lot of thinking about what your child likes. Maybe it's playing video games with you, a gift of art supplies, sleepovers with friends or an act of service such as taking over their chore for one day. Try making a list of incentives or rewards with your child. Ask them what some of their favorite rewards are. These may be rewards they can earn on a daily basis, like allowance or screen time, and even "bigger ticket" items that they could achieve over days or weeks.

When you add concrete rewards, they can serve to help you help your child keep her "eye on the prize." In this way, you are serving as her supportive coach during moments when she begins to digress. That builds relationship and can generate significant results.

So how exactly do tangible rewards work? The approach can be as varied as families and children are. There is no one right way to use rewards as motivation. Below, you will find several ideas we have found to motivate behavioral change using tangible rewards.

1. **Super Green Box**

Fill a box with small items your kids would like to receive. Candy, money, coins to collect towards something bigger, gum, small toys, or games. Keep one in the car and one at home, and use it to reward super green choices on the spot. Remember the benefit of intermittent reward. Not every time, and certainly not when they ask. Set up those guidelines ahead of time.

2. **Reward Cards and Charts**

Use 3X5 cards or your computer to create "coupons" that your kids can redeem. Use these as rewards for weekly or monthly rewards. Charts and coupons are available for download from several sites online. One of our favorites is: http://www.freeprintablebehaviorcharts.com.

3. **Point-Based Rewards System for Kids – Coin Jars**

A coin jar can be flexible and simple reward system that allows the child to choose what they wish to work towards from a menu that has been created together. For example, one child may be earning coins for doing chores without being asked, while another child is working toward to goal of being respectful by waiting their turn to talk rather than interrupting. The goals are specifically tailored to areas of growth for each individual child.

A variety of rewards are available for the child to choose from when redeeming the coins they earn. Each reward is assigned a point value or the number of coins they must accrue receive the reward. Coins may be used to reward green and super green behaviors or for doing chores and be applied to predetermined rewards. For example, your child's goal for the week may be doing chores without being asked. Each time they meet that expectation they receive five coins. A green behavior reward may be worth one coin and a super green behavior, worth five. They may be working toward a reward such as a trip to the Trampoline Zone that requires twenty-five coins. So each time they do chores without a reminder, you give them five coins to drop in the jar. In five days, they would earn twenty-five. You can see that you need to come up with the value in coins required to reach their goal. If they miss a day, they can make it up with green and super green behaviors, but that means you have to notice those behaviors and pay up.

4. **Super Green Hall of Fame**

Post a "hall of fame" on the wall—a place to put a picture of the child who has achieved super green for a designated period of time, such as one week. That way they are recognized an entire week by anyone coming through your home. Don't be afraid to have more than one child's picture in the hall of fame at a time. If you'd like to add a bonus to being placed into the super green hall of fame, you could always allow them to choose from a list of rewards like being able to choose dinner on Friday, or select the family fun activity for the following week. Or you could reward them with a specific number of coins.

> **Stop and Reflect**
>
> How good is your tangible reward system? If you already have one, how are you doing with setting goals with your kids and paying out on time? If you don't have a system, consider one of those mentioned above, sit down with your kids to set a goal or two and try the new system out.

Motivating Change through Rewards

None of us is perfect, and that goes for our kids too. We all have areas of behavior that are easy for us and other areas that are tough. Using a reward system to identify goals and reward progress is a great way to produce better habits in the long run. You have done a lot of thinking about how you can value and respect your child through your choice of rewards. Here a few things you can do to use your reward system most successfully:

1. **Keep a visual reminder of the reward system in front of you.**

    Post the chart or put the coin jar where you and the child will see it often. They need to see it so they are reminded of the goals. You need to see it every day so you are reminded to notice and reward the progress. Make sure you have chosen a system of rewards that you are able to maintain. Sticker charts, coin jars, or even tally marks on a while board are all ways you can track progress visually throughout the week. It is great to post the goal on the chart or jar.

2. **Make the goals attainable.**

    Post some goals on the chart or with your coin jar system that will allow your child to feel immediate success and then include goals that will stretch your child. Make sure the goals you decide are realistic and attainable for your child. Arrive at the goals together and make certain they are agreed on together. *For example*, "Follow direction the first time," may be an impossible goal for some kids, but "follow directions the first time at least 50 percent of the time" is a good stepping stone. Another way is to have them work toward following directions three times in a row. You want it to be concrete and tangible and setting a specific number of actions required makes it concrete rather than subjective.

    Make sure you include behavior goals as well as chore goals in your system. And reward systems are a great opportunity to work on character traits like kindness and generosity. Again, it will be helpful to have some goals that are easy for them to reach as well as those that stretch them.

3. **Make the rewards something your child sees as worth working toward.**

   Remember, this is not just something that you have decided is a good idea for your child to work toward. This is something that you have agreed on together. There may be times when your child has a gap that needs to be addressed and they don't feel willing or able to work on it. In those circumstances, let your child know the goal. Ask them if it seems doable; if not, be willing to make small adjustments, and let them know the good that you believe will come from them making progress in this area. Work with your child to figure out their currency and a reward that is meaningful to them. The best way to do this is to spend the time to make a list together that gives a number of different options.

4. **Be consistent: stick to it.**

   Rewards will only work when you are able to achieve enough consistency that the child can trust that you will follow through. Choose a time every week to "pay up" on the chart or the coin jar system. Also, set aside a minute each day to mark the chart or pay out the coins so you don't have to try and remember what happened over the whole week. If you practice noticing the good behavior on the spot, make the reward right then (coin or mark on the chart).

   Keep it simple so that you are able to be consistent. There are even phone apps that can help you keep track of points earned toward rewards: http://www.irewardchart.com/.

   You can do this.

   Whenever you can *both* reward behavior, and spend quality time together, *do it*. It builds lasting bonds that will benefit your family for generations to come!

Putting Reset Families into Practice in Five Minutes or Less:

- Review Reset—what is the best part and what is most challenging?
- Have a family meeting to talk about goals and rewards.
- If you decide to use a super green box, describe how they earn a "reach" into the box.
- Decide with the kids what type of reward system would work for your family. Write it down and begin to implement that.
- Set a short-term goal with each of your kids, and for the older kids, maybe a long-term goal. Maybe they want to earn money for a weekend trip with friends or a bicycle. First ask the kids what they think they need to do to earn that. Then decide on an appropriate reward together. Write it down and keep track so that you pay off.

Further Resources, Page 187

Afterword

On Being Human, Restoring Connections, and Painting Pictures of Hope

Throughout this book we have emphasized that the Reset Families approach to discipline will help you strengthen your family relationships as you teach your kids the skills to manage their own behavior. We've said that the starting point of effective discipline is building stronger relationships with your children. We've encouraged you to create a family culture that communicates value and worth to your kids. That they have a voice, that you are listening and want them to be part of the team.

You are teaching your kids that they can make mistakes, but it is not the end of the world. They are learning to own their behavior choices, think about a better plan for the future, and repair the damage so they can move on without the baggage of relational damage. As you teach your kids the redirection skills, not only are you giving them lifelong skills, it will make your interactions with your kids less stressful and more rewarding.

As you have identified your shared family vision, set aside time for family activities and to have intentional conversations, you have been painting pictures of hope for your family. Hope that you can continue to make change and move toward your family's hopes and dreams. As you carefully consider consequences that are related, reasonable, and restorative with our children, you are painting pictures of hope. Hope that your kids can trust that you will be consistent in helping them learn from their mistakes rather than merely punishing them.

Remember to paint pictures of hope for yourself. Hope that while you may not get it all right, your kids will benefit, even when you are sure you messed it up. Hope that they will hear your apologies and extend forgiveness, as you do the same with them. Hope that as you continue to use redirection, they will not only learn to manage their own behavior but will also see and experience the power of restoration. Paint the picture of hope that gives you and your kids' permission to start again to make meaningful change. That is the hope of Reset Families.

Further Resources

Chapter 1

Identify your parenting style:
https://psychcentral.com/quizzes/parenting-style-quiz/

Identify your child's love language:
https://www.5lovelanguages.com/profile/children/

Reflecting on Your Parenting

Session 1 – Change Starts with You!

1. Think about your parenting. What are you most proud of?

2. What is one thing you would like to change in your parenting style? What can you do this week to begin that change?

3. How would you describe your default parenting style? How do your kids react to that style?

4. Identify one stressful situation that might come up at home this week. Write an example of how you would like to speak or act in that situation rather than reacting from your default style.

Ten Ways to Improve Your Relationship through Mindfulness

1. Notice the impact you have on each other—note whatever is happening in the moment with a gentle and open mind
2. Pay attention to your child's facial expressions when you're saying something. Noticing how they are reacting to your words will help you communicate better
3. When you are at dinner, agree to put your electronic devices away—demonstrate our desire to give them your full attention, and ask the same from them.
4. When you are doing an activity like walking, designate part of the time to be in silence together, simply aware of sights and sounds. It makes it easier to speak honestly and openly.
5. Be present for the happy, fun moments, so they take priority. You don't want to miss out on the good stuff!
6. Respond rather than react in the angry, fearful moments. When the bad stuff comes, don't let your anger explode—instead, take a deep breath and respond thoughtfully.
7. Approach your child with curiosity so that you can continue to get to know him or her better. There is always more to discover and celebrate.

FURTHER RESOURCES

8. Be present for what your child is saying without jumping in immediately to solve his or her problem. Often, your presence listening is what your child needs more than your advice.
9. Relax and just listen. Good communication helps enable you to meet each other's needs and builds trust.
10. Being present for your child will help you feel more deeply connected, and you are showing them a pattern that they can follow.

Adapted from Cheryl Jones, Aetna's Mindfulness Center

Chapter 2

Family Assets Framework:
https://www.search-institute.org/wp-content/uploads/2018/02/Family_Assets_Framework.pdf

Tell Your Heart to Beat Again
https://www.youtube.com/watch?v=azYK8I2uoog

Developmental Relationships Framework
http://search-institute.org/downloadable/Developmental-Relationships-Framework.pdf

Developmental Assets
http://www.search-institute.org/developmental-assets/lists

Family Strengths
http://www.search-institute.org/research/family-strengths

Clarifying Family Hopes and Dreams

What are your hopes and dreams for your family? Use the following topics to organize your ideas. Imagine what it means to create a healthy family in each of the following areas:

Social

What do family relationships look like? What do outside relationships look like?

Emotional

How do you express emotions? How do you accept others' feelings?

What does it look like to be emotionally healthy?

Physical

What does physically healthy living look like? What activities do you want to include?

Spiritual

What do you want your family to know about spiritually? What traditions do you already have in place?

How do you look for help outside yourself?

Family Hopes and Dreams with Preschool-Age Children

Establishing family hopes and dreams gives us something to work toward together and we want kids of all ages to be a part of the process. This can be challenging with very young children, so here are some ideas to consider for including kids in a hopes and dreams project:

- *Make a tree.* Include them in finger-painting: handprints make great leaves on a tree (cut-up paper grocery bags work great for finger-painting on or for making a tree trunk!). When all your paint has dried, write your family hopes and dreams on the poster with a permanent marker.
- *Make a collage.* To simplify, have kids cut construction paper into different shapes and sizes. Use these to write your family hopes and dreams on. Paste them on your poster. (Kids *love* being in charge of glue sticks or telling

you where to put things next. Adding some puff balls, buttons, or stickers from the dollar store can also be fun.)
- Remember, this is just as much about the *process* of thinking through things you want in your family and in your future, as it is about the *finished product*. So let kids have fun with it.
- *Keep it short and sweet*, so kids can be engaged and stay excited about the project. Even if kids are too young to process "hopes and dreams" they can have a sense of pride and ownership of a poster that they helped glue or paint. This may mean you do more ahead of time and just let them assemble.
- For kids who are more verbal, or a little older, ask prompt questions to *add a few of their own ideas*. For example, "What should our home be like?" "What kind of family do you *wish* we could be?" "What do you want to be when you grow up?" "What do you really hope might happen in the future?"
- *Have fun!* And remember, if making the poster is a positive experience, your child will enjoy looking at it and be reminded of what is important to your family.

Creating a Shared Family Vision: Alternate Activity

Tribute Letter

Fast forward your life to a future scene. Your child, now nineteen, has just arrived home from college to join you for Thanksgiving and presents you with a tribute letter. This is to thank you for the ways you have invested in him/her over the past years.

Take the time to write the message you would like to hear in this tribute letter, including description of the relationship, what they value and the memories they have.

Let your imagination go wild. Do not limit yourself by what you think is possible—or what you are experiencing now . . . Write your hopes and dreams.

Chapter 3

Visit www.resetfamilies.org and search for Check-in Activity Sheet
Visit www.resetfamilies.org and search for Emotion Chart
Self-Control Games: https://www.youtube.com/watch?v=H_O1brYwdSY

Family Connection Planning

1. **Make a Plan**

Date:

Time:

Cost:

Snacks:

Who is responsible? _____

2. **Check In: (select from check-in activity list provided)**

Who picks the activity? _____
Who leads the activity? _____

3. **Set the Ground Rules**

4. **Have Intentional Conversations**

What is the topic? _____
Who will lead the discussion? _____

5. **Choose a Family Activity**

What will we do? _____

6. **Assign Tasks**

Who is responsible for what?

7. **Clarify Expectations**

What rules will help us all have a good time?

Ground Rules

1. Everyone gets a chance to talk.
2. One person talks at a time.
3. It's okay to say what you feel—use "I" statements.
4. No one has to talk.
5. Everyone has to listen.
6. No one puts anyone else down.
7. _____
8. _____
9. _____

Chapter 4

Family Rules

1. _____
2. _____
3. _____
4. _____
5. _____
6. _____
7. _____
8. _____
9. _____
10. _____
11. _____
12. _____
13. _____
14. _____
15. _____
16. _____
17. _____
18. _____
19. _____
20. _____

FURTHER RESOURCES

Family Expectations

1. **Be Respectful** – Respect is about valuing another person as well as yourself.

2. **Be Responsible** – Responsibility is about taking care of the things that are within your power, control, or ability to manage.

3. **Be a Listener** – Listening is not only about hearing, but also about processing information, engaging, and following directions.

4. **Be Safe** – Safety if about keeping yourself and others from harm physically as well as guarding your heart and mind from things that might threaten your emotional, social, or spiritual health.

5. **Be Trustworthy** – Trustworthiness is about being honest, reliable, and dependable.

Setting Behavior Expectations

1. What behavior would you like to change?

2. What would happen instead? (Identify which of the five family expectations is most related.)

State your expectation in clear, explicit, concrete terms:

Ideas for Reflection

3. How would a change like this do to move you closer to your hopes and dreams?

4. What are obstacles that stand in your way? What are some reasonable paths around those obstacles?

Behavior Choices

Helping others with chores
Harming yourself or others
Reminding others of expectations (respectfully)
Refusing to follow directions
Distracting others during family conversation
Following directions
Showing good sportsmanship
Throwing furniture
Cutting in line
Teasing others
Trying your hardest at a new activity
Touching inappropriately
Showing compassion
Staying with your family at an outing
Cursing
Hiding
Cleaning without being asked
Lying
Doing what you're asked
Bullying
Complimenting/encouraging others
Teasing
Being a team player
Roughhousing
Making violent threats
Sharing without prompting
Refusing to follow directions
Being on-task
Using a weapon to threaten
Defacing property

Participating
Pouting and whining
Throwing things (without intent to harm)
Acting out sexually
Having a good attitude
Standing on chairs or table
Using drugs or alcohol
Wandering from your family at an outing
Being rude—farting or belching
Taking a break instead of reacting in anger
Cleaning up after themselves
Arguing with sibling
Refusing to do homework
Getting ready for bed on time
Biting, pinching, spitting or hitting
Respecting others' personal space
Name-calling
Making excuses or blaming others for mistake

Chapter 5

Visit www.resetfamilies.org and search for Self-Management Repair Chart

Scenarios

Choose appropriate scenarios for each of the discussions for this session.

Use Redirection and/or Reset to coach the child. Practice around your tables.

RESET FAMILIES

1. Six-year-old is playing Angry Birds on the iPad. Mother gives him a two-minute warning to finish game and come and help set the table.

    a. Son finishes game and comes directly to set table.
    b. Son ignores request—practice using step 1/2 of redirection.
    c. After first nonverbal cue, son says, "No, I have to finish my game."
    d. Child is compliant after second cue—the precision request.
    e. Child continues to ignore—take through reset.
    f. Suggest consequences for child who is compliant after the second cue, for the child who refuses and goes thorough reset.

2. Twelve-year-old arrives home from school with family. He is instructed to hang up coat, take twenty minutes to relax, then get his homework done.

    a. Throws coat and bag on floor and sits down to text a friend.
    b. Puts coat and bag away, says he is going to room to do homework, and Dad finds him texting a friend rather than doing homework.

3. Thirteen-year-old is frustrated and angry at his eight-year-old sister who won't leave him alone and let him text. What do you do in each of the scenarios?

    a. Thirteen-year-old calls her a name and pushes her away.
    b. Eight-year-old pushes him back as she screams and cries and pretends to be hurt.

FURTHER RESOURCES

Chapter 6

For Preschool, Elementary and Youth Reset Sheets visit www.reset-families.org and search for Reset Sheets

Chapter 7

Come up with Some Natural Consequences

- Soccer ball is kicked around in the house.
- A four-year-old refuses to pick up her dolls.
- Child goes outside without a hat in the snow.
- An eight-year-old child rides his bike out of the driveway.
- Teenager wants to stay up late.
- A ten-year-old is throwing a ball in the house, and he breaks a lamp.
- Child leaves toy outside.
- A six-year-old is coloring a picture on the coffee table and keeps coloring on the table instead of her paper.
- Child wants to spend money on something you think is frivolous.
- A nine-year-old misses the bus on purpose.
- Child cheats on a game.
- A seven-year-old refuses to eat his dinner.

Below are some "natural" consequences:

- Soccer ball is kicked around in the house. Consequence example: the soccer ball that's always getting kicked in the house will go on time out.
- A four-year-old refuses to pick up her dolls. Consequence example: she loses her privileges to play with the dolls for the rest of the day.
- Child goes outside without a hat in the snow. Consequence example: allow child to go outside without a hat as long as

it is not dangerously cold. He'll feel cold and return to find a solution.
- An eight-year-old child rides his bike out of the driveway. Consequence example: loses his bicycle privileges for twenty-four hours.
- Teenager wants to stay up late. Consequence example: allow a teenager to set his own bedtime. If he stays up too late he'll feel tired the next morning. Then when he is late for school, he loses the privilege until he can be responsible.
- A ten-year-old is throwing a ball in the house and he breaks a lamp. Consequence example: he has to do chores to earn enough money to pay for a new lamp.
- Child leaves toy outside. Consequence example: Depending on the value, allow a child to leave a toy outside. The parent may choose to put it undercover and give the child the opportunity to pay them back for taking responsibility for their toy, or they may choose to let it get ruined.
- A six-year-old is coloring a picture on the coffee table and keeps coloring on the table after being reminded, instead of her paper. Consequence example: She loses the crayons for the rest of the day.
- Child wants to spend money on something you think is frivolous. Consequence example: Allow a child to spend some of his money. He may not have enough money to do another activity with his friends.
- A nine-year-old misses the bus on purpose. Consequence example: His mother drives him to school, but he has to do chores to earn gas money to pay for the ride to school and also has to stay after school to make up for the time he missed in the morning.
- Child cheats on a game. Consequence example: His brother doesn't want to play with him anymore.
- A seven-year-old refuses to eat his dinner. Consequence example: he's not allowed to have desert or a snack before bed.

Chapter 8

Coupon Examples
visit www.resetfamilies.org and search for Reward Coupons.
Phone App for Rewards: www.irewardschart.com
Reward Charts: www.kidsrewardchart.com

Points-Based Rewards System for Kids

Rationale

1. Kids are motivated to modify their behavior when there is a reward offered.
2. However, parents do not always know what it is the kids want. Or the rewards offered involve spending a lot of money.
3. If a child can choose their reward, they will choose the thing they want most.
4. A rewards system should be flexible and simple.
5. A parent wants to do nice things for their kids.

The system:

1. *Reward children with points for doing things that you want them to do.*
   a. Chores
   b. Reading books
   c. Playing outside
   d. Getting caught doing something good

2. *Use a physical token (like poker chips).*
    a. Helps children to budget and save
    b. Is countable
    c. Is tangible
    d. Is easily traded
    e. Makes a satisfying "clink" when it is dropped in a jar
    f. Can be awarded with some ceremony

3. *Decide how many points to give as a reward.*
    a. We use multiples of five.
    b. Every chore or desired behavior is rewarded with five points.
    c. Increase point values for bigger tasks, or just because you want to.

4. *Make a menu of rewards.*

(We decided to make a list of things we would have let the children do anyway, just because we like them. But now there are natural limits on things like video games or TV because the children end up spending their points. Once the points are gone, the TV or game is shut off. We also set an upper limit to the amount of TV or video games that can be bought in a day.)

   a. Each item on the menu has a point value attached.
   b. Video games and TV are one point per minute with an upper limit of forty minutes per day.
   c. Trip to the store is eighty points. (That is just transport to the store, the child needs to spend their own money when they are there. We do not charge a child to go to the store if they are accompanying us on errands, as we are at the store anyway . . .)
   d. Trip to the pool – 150 points.
   e. Fishing – 200 points.
   f. Picnic lunch on the lawn – 75 points.
   g. You can think of all kinds of things to let children do, but that can be a reward because they choose to invest their points in buying the activity.

Other Thoughts

The beauty of this system is that screen time is limited, and children do a lot of the limiting themselves. They skip the video game because they are saving points to go to the store to spend their allowance. They read extra books or play outside to earn points to play a game. (We reward twenty minutes of outside play with five points. The more they play outside, the more points they get, but we end up far ahead because they spend four times as much time outside than they do on screen time.)

Adjusting the system is easy. Being consistent is important. Reward good behavior quickly, it is too easy to lose track otherwise. Don't have children go grab their points to put in their jar. This leads to too much temptation to grab twenty instead of five. We learned that the hard way and had to be watchful of inter sibling point theft.

References

1. http://www.pbis.org/
2. Patterson, Gerald L. 1982. *Coercive Family Process.* Oregon: Casgtalia Publishing Company.
3. Yerkovick, Milan and Kay. 2011. *How We Love Our Kids.* Colorado: Waterbrook Press.
4. Siegel, Daniel J. 2010. "About Interpersonal Neurobiology: An Introduction to Interpersonal Neurobiology" Retrieved from www.drdansiegel.com/about/interpersonal_nuerobiology/.
5. Taylor, Jim. 2011. *Your Children Are Listening: Nine Messages They Need to Hear from You.* New York: The Experiment Publishing.
6. Family Assets. 2012. Search Institute. Retrieved from https://www.searchinstitute.org/wpcontent/uploads/2018/02/Family_Assets_Framework.pdf.
7. Gokey, Daniel. 2014. "Tell Your Heart to Beat Again." "Hope in Front of Me." Tennessee: BMG. https://www.youtube.com/watch?v=azYK8I2uoog.
8. Gottman, John. M. 1997. *Raising an Emotionally Intelligent Child: The Heart of Parenting.* New York, NY: Fireside Press.
9. Chapin, Harry. 1974. "Cat's in the Cradle." "Verities and Balderdash." Connecticut: Connecticut Recording Studios.
10. Greenberg, Mark, Siegel, Judith. M., and Leitsch, Cynthia J. 1983. "The Nature and Importance of Attachment Relationships to Parents and Peers during Adolescence." *Journal of Youth and Adolescence.* 12(5). 373-386.
11. Cambridge Dictionary of American English Bribe. 2007. "Bribe." Accessed May 10, 2108. https://dictionary.cambridge.org/us/dictionary/english/bribe.

[12] Oxford English Dictionary. 2013. "Reward." Accessed May 10, 2018. https://en.oxforddictionaries.com/definition/reward.
[13] Chapman, Gary D. and Campbell, Ross. 2016. *The Five Love Languages of Children.* Illinois: Northfield Publishing.
[14] Dweck, Carol S. 2016. *Mindset: The New Psychology of Success.* New York: Ballantine Books.

About the Authors

Sharon Aller, DTL, has had a lifelong commitment to the needs of families. She has spent much of her adult life creating connections between parents and their communities, providing practical tools, and creating networks that encourage families on their parenting journey. She served as executive director of a community agency for the past ten years helping vulnerable families navigate behavioral and emotional challenges. She conducts workshops for parents, educators, and clinicians. She lives near Blaine, Washington, with her husband, Warren, and shares in the lives of her adult children and grandchildren. She recently completed doctoral work in transformational leadership and piloted a Reset Families curriculum for use by schools and a variety of community agencies.

Gregory J. Benner, PhD, is a Helen and Pat O'Sullivan Endowed Professor, Special Education and Multiple Abilities at the University of Alabama–Tuscaloosa. Dr. Benner specializes in preventive, systemic, and sustainable approaches for meeting the needs of the whole child, particularly those with emotional and behavioral disorders. He has a knack for collective impact—getting whole communities including families, child welfare, mental health, and schools on the same page to meet needs of the whole child. His book, titled *Instructional Practices for Students with Behavioral Disorders: Strategies for Reading, Writing, and Math*, is part of the What Works for Special Needs Learners Series published by Guilford Press. He has a strong track record of sponsored research; serving as Principal Investigator on an Institute of Education Sciences (IES) funded Efficacy Study (R324A07183) from 2007 to 2011 and currently as PI on an IES funded Development and Innovation Study (R324A150059). He is an Associate Editor for behavioral disorders and on the editorial review board for the Journal of Emotional and Behavioral Disorders. He has over 250 presentations and publications that reflect his ability to disseminate research findings and best practices to the field.

Angel Finsrud has spent her life investing in children and families. Though she has a degree in social sciences, her greatest teachers have been the children and parents she has walked along side as a foster parent for more than thirteen years. As a speaker, trainer, and teacher she is passionate about equipping and inspiring people. Angel lives with her husband, Kevin, in Bellingham, Washington, where life is an adventure with their five children, including three adopted.

CPSIA information can be obtained
at www.ICGtesting.com
Printed in the USA
FFHW02n1436041018
48671821-52677FF